Essential Mediterranean Diet Cookbook for Beginners

Your Guide to Effortless Preparation and Flavorful Life with 150+ Healthful Recipes and 30-Day Meal Plan

Andrea Motley

In this recipe book you will find:

The nutritional information for each recipe is given per serving

To the vibrant cultures of the Mediterranean, whose rich traditions and love for simple, wholesome food continue to inspire the world.

And to my family and friends, whose shared meals and warm conversations remind me every day that food is more than nourishment—it's connection, celebration, and love.

Introduction

Welcome to the vibrant and flavorful world of Mediterranean cuisine! As someone who has spent the last eight years living in France, I have been fortunate to immerse myself in the rich culinary traditions of the Mediterranean. My love for this cuisine runs deep, and over time, it has become an integral part of my daily life. From the fresh markets of Provence to the coastal flavors of Greece, Italy, Turkey, and Morocco, I've come to appreciate the simplicity, healthfulness, and pure joy that Mediterranean cooking brings to the table.

My journey with Mediterranean food began as a passion and has since transformed into a lifestyle. Living in France has only deepened my appreciation for the way these flavors can seamlessly blend into everyday meals, making cooking both nourishing and exciting. The Mediterranean diet is not just about following a set of recipes—it's about embracing a way of eating that is balanced, flavorful, and rooted in fresh, wholesome ingredients.

In this book, I'm excited to share with you a collection of dishes that celebrate the essence of Mediterranean cuisine. These recipes are not only delicious but also reflect the way I eat on a daily basis—whether it's a simple breakfast drizzled with olive oil, a vibrant salad packed with vegetables, or a comforting soup filled with legumes and herbs. Each dish highlights the beauty of using quality ingredients, many of which you can find in your local market, no matter where you are.

What I love most about Mediterranean cooking is how it brings people together. There is a certain magic in sharing a meal with loved ones, where the food becomes a centerpiece for connection, laughter, and warmth. Through these recipes, I hope to inspire you to embrace the Mediterranean way of eating—not just as a diet but as a way of life that is joyful, sustainable, and deeply satisfying.

So, whether you're new to Mediterranean cuisine or a seasoned home cook looking for fresh inspiration, this book is for you. I hope it fills your kitchen with vibrant flavors and brings a sense of Mediterranean sunshine to your everyday meals, just as it has to mine.

Bon appétit,

Andrea Motley

What is the Mediterranean Diet?

The Mediterranean Diet is more than just a way of eating—it's a lifestyle celebrated for its health benefits, delicious flavors, and cultural richness. Originating from the Mediterranean region, this dietary pattern has captivated the world, emphasizing fresh, whole foods and simple yet flavorful cooking techniques.

Introduction to the Mediterranean Diet

The Mediterranean Diet is not a restrictive regimen but a flexible and inclusive approach to nourishing the body and soul. At its core, it encourages the consumption of plant-based foods, healthy fats, lean proteins, and a moderate intake of wine—all inspired by the traditional diets of countries bordering the Mediterranean Sea.

In the Mediterranean Diet, fresh fruits and vegetables take center stage, providing a rainbow of colors, flavors, and nutrients. These seasonal treasures are complemented by whole grains, legumes, and nuts, forming the foundation of wholesome meals. Olive oil, a symbol of the Mediterranean lifestyle, is the primary source of fat, cherished for its rich flavor and abundance of heart-healthy monounsaturated fats.

Lean proteins such as poultry, fish, and seafood are enjoyed in moderation, while dairy products like Greek yogurt and cheese add richness and tanginess to dishes. Fresh herbs and spices elevate the aroma and flavor of Mediterranean cuisine, offering a symphony of tastes that delight the senses.

A Brief History of the Diet Across Various Mediterranean Countries

The Mediterranean Diet is not a monolithic concept but a tapestry woven from the diverse culinary traditions of the countries bordering the Mediterranean Sea. Each region contributes unique flavors, ingredients, and cultural practices to this celebrated way of eating.

Greece

In Greece, the Mediterranean Diet finds its roots in ancient times, where a diet rich in olive oil, grains, fruits, vegetables, and fish sustained the people of Crete and other regions. The concept of "meze," small plates of appetizers shared among friends and family, is integral to Greek dining culture.

Italy

Italy's contribution to the Mediterranean Diet is unmistakable, with its emphasis on fresh produce, pasta, tomatoes, olive oil, and aromatic herbs. Italian cuisine varies from region to region, reflecting the diversity of landscapes and culinary traditions across the country.

Spain

Spain's Mediterranean Diet is characterized by vibrant flavors and a love for bold spices and ingredients. Paella, gazpacho, and tapas are iconic dishes that showcase the bounty of Spain's land and sea. The tradition of the siesta—a midday break for rest—emphasizes the importance of balance and enjoying meals at a leisurely pace.

France

France's contribution to the Mediterranean Diet is exemplified by the cuisine of Provence, where olive oil, garlic, tomatoes, and aromatic herbs like rosemary and thyme reign supreme. French dining culture places a strong emphasis on quality ingredients, seasonal produce, and savoring meals with good company.

Türkiye

Turkey's rich culinary heritage blends elements of Mediterranean, Middle Eastern, and Central Asian cuisines. Turkish cuisine features an abundance of fresh vegetables, grains, legumes, and lean meats, often seasoned with fragrant spices like cumin, coriander, and sumac.

Lebanon

Lebanon's Mediterranean Diet is characterized by its mezze culture, where a colorful array of small dishes is served to be shared and enjoyed communally. Hummus, tabbouleh, falafel, and grilled meats are staples of Lebanese cuisine, showcasing the flavors of the Mediterranean with a Middle Eastern twist.

The Mediterranean Diet is a testament to the rich cultural heritage and culinary creativity of the diverse communities that call the Mediterranean region home. By exploring the history and traditions of each country, we gain a deeper appreciation for the flavors and ingredients that make the Mediterranean Diet a beloved and enduring culinary tradition.

Description of the Diet's Primary Components and Food Groups

The Mediterranean Diet is characterized by its emphasis on fresh, whole foods and simple yet flavorful cooking techniques. Understanding the diet's primary components and food groups is key to embracing this wholesome way of eating.

Plant-Based Foods

Fruits, vegetables, whole grains, legumes, and nuts form the cornerstone of the Mediterranean Diet. These nutrient-rich foods provide a plethora of vitamins, minerals, fiber, and antioxidants essential for good health. Incorporating a variety of colorful fruits and vegetables into your meals ensures a diverse range of nutrients and flavors.

Healthy Fats

Olive oil is the quintessential fat of the Mediterranean Diet, prized for its rich flavor and abundance of monounsaturated fats. Other sources of healthy fats include nuts, seeds, and fatty fish like salmon and mackerel. These fats contribute to heart health, satiety, and the absorption of fat-soluble vitamins.

Lean Proteins

Poultry, fish, and seafood are primary sources of protein in the Mediterranean Diet. These lean protein sources provide essential amino acids for muscle repair and maintenance. Legumes such as beans, lentils, and chickpeas are also excellent sources of plant-based protein, fiber, and complex carbohydrates.

Dairy Products:

Greek yogurt and cheese are enjoyed in moderation in the Mediterranean Diet, providing calcium, protein, and probiotics. Greek yogurt is a versatile ingredient in both sweet and savory dishes, while cheese adds richness and flavor to Mediterranean recipes.

Herbs and Spices

Fresh herbs and spices are used liberally in Mediterranean cooking to enhance the aroma and flavor of dishes. Basil, parsley, mint, oregano, and cilantro are just a few examples of herbs commonly used in Mediterranean cuisine. Spices like cumin, coriander, paprika, and cinnamon add depth and complexity to recipes, without the need for excess salt or unhealthy condiments.

Occasional Treats

Red wine and sweets are enjoyed occasionally and in moderation as part of the Mediterranean Diet. Red wine, in particular, is rich in antioxidants and polyphenols, which may offer health benefits when consumed in moderation. Desserts featuring fruit, nuts, and honey provide a sweet ending to meals without compromising on flavor or nutrition.

By understanding the primary components and food groups of the Mediterranean Diet, you can embark on a culinary journey that nourishes both body and soul. Embrace the abundance of plant-based foods, savor the flavors of healthy fats and lean proteins, and indulge in occasional treats with mindfulness and moderation. With each meal, celebrate the vibrant colors, bold flavors, and cultural richness of the Mediterranean region.

Core Principles of the Mediterranean Lifestyle

The Mediterranean Diet is a holistic approach to health and well-being that encompasses the way you live, eat, and interact with others. Understanding the core principles of the Mediterranean lifestyle is essential for embracing this enriching way of life.

Importance of Meal Timing and Social Meals

In the Mediterranean culture, mealtime is cherished as a time for connection, celebration, and nourishment. Unlike hurried meals on the go, Mediterranean meals are enjoyed slowly and savored with family and friends. This social aspect of dining fosters a sense of community and belonging, contributing to overall well-being.

Meal timing in the Mediterranean lifestyle follows a natural rhythm, with breakfast, lunch, and dinner being the main meals of the day. Breakfast is typically light but nutritious, providing energy to start the day. Lunch is the largest meal, enjoyed leisurely with coworkers or family members. Dinner is a lighter affair, allowing the body to digest before bedtime. Eating together as a family or with loved ones promotes mindful eating and healthy food choices. Sharing meals creates opportunities for conversation, laughter, and bonding, strengthening relationships and fostering a sense of unity. In the Mediterranean tradition, mealtime isn't just about nourishing the body—it's about feeding the soul.

Active Lifestyle that Complements the Diet

The Mediterranean lifestyle extends beyond the dining table to embrace an active way of life. Physical activity is woven into daily routines, whether it's walking to the market, tending to the garden, or enjoying outdoor recreational activities. Regular exercise not only promotes physical health but also enhances mood, reduces stress, and improves overall quality of life.

In the Mediterranean region, walking is a primary mode of transportation, allowing people to stay active as they go about their daily lives. This emphasis on movement and physical activity contributes to lower rates of obesity, heart disease, and other chronic conditions.

Engaging in outdoor activities such as hiking, swimming, and cycling provides opportunities to connect with nature and enjoy the beautiful landscapes of the Mediterranean region. Whether it's a stroll along the coast or a challenging hike in the mountains, staying active is an integral part of the Mediterranean lifestyle.

By incorporating regular physical activity into your daily routine, you can complement the healthy eating habits of the Mediterranean Diet and reap the numerous benefits of an active lifestyle. Embrace movement as a joyful expression of vitality and well-being, and let it enrich your journey toward optimal health and happiness.

Seasonality and Sustainability

In the Mediterranean lifestyle, eating with the seasons and embracing sustainability are fundamental principles that honor the natural rhythms of the earth and promote environmental stewardship. By prioritizing seasonal, locally sourced ingredients and adopting eco-friendly practices, you can reduce your carbon footprint and support the health of the planet.

Eating with the Seasons

Seasonal eating is deeply ingrained in Mediterranean culture, with meals centered around the freshest fruits, vegetables, and herbs available each season. By choosing produce that is in season, you not only enjoy peak flavor and nutritional quality but also support local farmers and reduce the environmental impact of long-distance transportation. Eating with the seasons encourages diversity in your diet and fosters a deeper connection to the natural world.

Embracing Sustainability

The Mediterranean lifestyle values sustainability as a way of life, recognizing the interconnectedness between human health and the health of the planet. Sustainable practices such as organic farming, regenerative agriculture, and responsible fishing methods are integral to preserving the delicate ecosystems of the Mediterranean region. By choosing sustainably sourced ingredients and minimizing food waste, you can contribute to a more resilient and sustainable food system for future generations.

Reducing Food Waste

In the Mediterranean kitchen, resourcefulness is key, and nothing goes to waste. Leftover ingredients are repurposed into new dishes, vegetable scraps are used to make flavorful stocks and broths, and even stale bread is transformed into delicious dishes like Panzanella or breadcrumbs. By embracing a "nose-to-tail" and "root-to-stem" approach to cooking, you can minimize food waste and maximize the value of every ingredient.

Connecting with the Earth

In addition to nourishing the body, the Mediterranean lifestyle emphasizes the importance of connecting with the Earth and appreciating the beauty and bounty of nature. Whether it's tending to a garden, visiting a local farmers' market, or enjoying a stroll through the countryside, spending time in nature cultivates a sense of gratitude and mindfulness, enhancing overall well-being.

Seasonality and sustainability are core principles of the Mediterranean lifestyle that promote harmony with nature, respect for the environment, and a deeper appreciation for the food we eat. By embracing these principles in your own life, you can nourish both body and soul while contributing to a healthier, more sustainable world for generations to come.

Health Benefits

The Mediterranean Diet isn't just about delicious food—it's also renowned for its numerous health benefits. From promoting heart health to supporting weight management and cognitive function, embracing the Mediterranean lifestyle can lead to a happier, healthier you.

Heart Health

One of the most well-known benefits of the Mediterranean Diet is its positive impact on heart health. The diet's emphasis on healthy fats, such as olive oil and fatty fish, along with an abundance of fruits, vegetables, and whole grains, can help lower LDL cholesterol levels and reduce the risk of heart disease. Studies have shown that adhering to the Mediterranean Diet can significantly decrease the incidence of heart attacks, strokes, and other cardiovascular events.

Weight Management

The Mediterranean Diet isn't a fad diet focused on deprivation—it's a sustainable way of eating that promotes balanced nutrition and portion control. With its emphasis on whole, nutrient-dense foods and moderation in indulgences, the Mediterranean Diet can support healthy weight loss and weight management. By nourishing the body with satisfying meals rich in fiber, protein, and healthy fats, you can feel satiated while achieving and maintaining a healthy weight.

Brain Health

Research suggests that the Mediterranean Diet may also benefit cognitive function and brain health. The diet's anti-inflammatory properties, thanks to its emphasis on antioxidants and omega-3 fatty acids, may help protect against age-related cognitive decline and neurodegenerative diseases such as Alzheimer's. Additionally, the Mediterranean lifestyle, which includes regular physical activity and social engagement, further contributes to brain health and overall well-being.

Longevity

One of the most fascinating aspects of the Mediterranean Diet is its association with longevity. Studies have shown that populations in Mediterranean countries tend to live longer and enjoy a higher quality of life compared to other regions. By following the principles of the Mediterranean Diet—eating a variety of nutrient-rich foods, staying physically active, and fostering strong social connections—you can increase your chances of living a longer, healthier life.

The health benefits of the Mediterranean Diet extend far beyond the dinner table, impacting every aspect of your well-being, from your heart to your brain to your overall longevity. By embracing the Mediterranean lifestyle and savoring the delicious flavors of Mediterranean cuisine, you can nourish your body and soul while enjoying a lifetime of vibrant health and happiness.

Adapting to the Mediterranean Diet

Transitioning to the Mediterranean Diet doesn't have to be daunting—it's about embracing a lifestyle that celebrates delicious, wholesome foods and nourishes both body and soul. With some practical tips and creative modifications, you can easily incorporate Mediterranean eating habits into your daily life and enjoy the vibrant flavors of this beloved culinary tradition.

Practical Tips for Incorporating Mediterranean Eating Habits into Daily Life

Start with Small Changes

Begin by gradually changing your diet rather than trying to overhaul your eating habits overnight. Start incorporating more fruits, vegetables, whole grains, and healthy fats into your meals, and gradually reduce processed foods and added sugars.

Experiment with New Ingredients

Explore the wide array of ingredients used in Mediterranean cuisine, from fresh herbs and spices to whole grains and legumes. Experiment with different flavors and textures to discover new favorite dishes and adapt traditional recipes to suit your taste preferences.

Cook at Home More Often

Cooking at home allows you to have more control over the ingredients you use and the cooking methods employed. Try preparing Mediterranean-inspired meals from scratch using fresh, seasonal ingredients, and involve family members or friends in the cooking process for a fun and interactive experience.

Focus on Plant-Based Foods

Center your meals around plant-based foods such as fruits, vegetables, legumes, nuts, and seeds. Aim to fill half your plate with colorful produce, and incorporate beans, lentils, and whole grains as hearty and satisfying alternatives to meat.

Use Olive Oil Liberally

Swap out butter and margarine for heart-healthy olive oil in cooking and dressing recipes. Extra virgin olive oil adds richness and flavor to dishes while providing essential monounsaturated fats and antioxidants.

Suggestions for Modifying Existing Recipes to Fit the Diet's Principles

Reduce Saturated Fats

Modify recipes that call for butter or heavy cream by using olive oil or Greek yogurt as healthier alternatives. Replace fatty cuts of meat with leaner options like poultry or fish, or incorporate more plant-based proteins such as beans or tofu.

Boost Flavor with Herbs and Spices

Enhance the flavor of dishes by incorporating fresh herbs and spices instead of relying on salt or processed seasonings. Experiment with Mediterranean herbs like basil, oregano, rosemary, and thyme to add depth and complexity to your meals.

Add More Vegetables

Amp up the nutritional value of recipes by adding extra vegetables wherever possible. Sneak finely chopped vegetables into sauces, soups, and casseroles, or bulk up salads and stir-fries with an assortment of colorful veggies.

Swap Grains for Whole Grains

Replace refined grains like white rice and pasta with whole grains such as brown rice, quinoa, barley, or whole wheat pasta. Whole grains are higher in fiber and nutrients, keeping you feeling full and satisfied for longer.

Focus on Fresh, Seasonal Ingredients

Choose recipes that feature fresh, seasonal ingredients, and adapt them to fit the availability of produce in your area. Opt for local and organic ingredients whenever possible to support sustainability and reduce environmental impact.

Adapting to the Mediterranean Diet is all about making simple, sustainable changes to your eating habits and embracing the vibrant flavors of Mediterranean cuisine. By incorporating practical tips and creative modifications into your daily life, you can enjoy the delicious and healthful benefits of this time-honored way of eating.

Olive Oil and Tomato Toast

INGREDIENTS

- 4 slices of whole-grain bread
- 2 large ripe tomatoes, sliced
- 4 teaspoons of extra virgin olive oil
- 1/2 teaspoon of sea salt
- 1/4 teaspoon of freshly ground black pepper
- Optional: 1/4 cup crumbled feta cheese
- Optional: Fresh basil leaves for garnish

 Prep Time: 10 min

 Cook Time: 5 min

 Serves: 4

DIRECTIONS

Toast the bread slices to your desired crispness in a toaster or under a broiler.
Arrange sliced tomatoes evenly over the toasted bread slices.
Drizzle each slice with 1 teaspoon of olive oil. Sprinkle salt and pepper evenly over the slices.
If using, sprinkle crumbled feta cheese on top of the tomatoes.
Garnish with fresh basil leaves, if desired, and serve immediately.

Nutritional Information: 180 calories, 5g protein, 20g carbohydrates, 9g fat, 3g fiber, 5mg cholesterol, 320mg sodium, 230mg potassium.

Grilled Halloumi Cheese with Lemon

INGREDIENTS

- 8 ounces halloumi cheese, sliced into 1/2-inch thick pieces
- 2 tablespoons olive oil
- 1 lemon, halved
- Freshly ground black pepper
- Optional: Fresh mint leaves for garnish

 Prep Time: 5 min

 Cook Time: 10 min

 Serves: 4

DIRECTIONS

Preheat a grill or grill pan over medium-high heat. Brush the halloumi slices lightly with olive oil on both sides.
Place the halloumi slices on the grill. Cook for about 3-4 minutes on each side, or until grill marks appear and the cheese is golden brown.
Squeeze lemon over the grilled halloumi and season with black pepper.
Serve immediately, garnished with fresh mint leaves if desired.

Nutritional Information: 273 calories, 16g protein, 2g carbohydrates, 22g fat, 0g fiber, 0mg cholesterol, 1070mg sodium, 25mg potassium.

Shakshuka (Eggs Poached in Tomato Sauce)

INGREDIENTS

- 1 tablespoon olive oil
- 1 medium onion, finely chopped
- 1 bell pepper, seeded and diced
- 3 cloves garlic, minced
- 2 teaspoons paprika
- 1 teaspoon cumin
- 1/4 teaspoon chili powder (adjust to taste)
- 1 can crushed tomatoes
- Salt and pepper to taste
- 4 large eggs
- Optional: Chopped cilantro or parsley for garnish

Prep Time: 15 min

Cook Time: 20 min

Serves: 4

DIRECTIONS

Heat olive oil in a large skillet over medium heat. Add onion and bell pepper, sautéing until softened, about 5 minutes. Add garlic and cook for 1 minute more. Stir in paprika, cumin, and chili powder, cooking for 1 minute until fragrant. Pour in crushed tomatoes and season with salt and pepper. Simmer the sauce for 10 minutes, allowing it to thicken slightly. Make four wells in the sauce with the back of a spoon. Crack an egg into each well. Cover the skillet and cook over low heat until the eggs are set, about 7-10. Garnish with cilantro or parsley if desired. Serve directly from the skillet with crusty bread on the side.

Nutritional Information: 235 calories, 11g protein, 25g carbohydrates, 11g fat, 6g fiber, 186mg cholesterol, 587mg sodium, 639mg potassium.

Tomato & Olive Tapenade on Whole Grain Bread

INGREDIENTS

- 4 slices of whole-grain bread
- 1/2 cup olive tapenade
- 2 medium tomatoes, sliced
- Optional: Fresh basil leaves for garnish

Prep Time: 10 min

Cook Time: 0 min

Serves: 4

DIRECTIONS

Toast the whole grain bread slices until golden and crispy.
Spread a generous layer of olive tapenade on each slice of toasted bread.
Top each slice with several tomato slices. Arrange neatly to cover the surface.
Garnish with fresh basil leaves if desired, and serve immediately.

Nutritional Information: 180 calories, 5g protein, 20g carbohydrates, 9g fat, 4g fiber, 0mg cholesterol, 410mg sodium, 300mg potassium.

Spinach and Feta Phyllo Pie

INGREDIENTS

- 1/2 cup olive oil
- 10 sheets of phyllo dough, thawed
- 1 onion, finely chopped
- 2 cloves garlic, minced
- 10 ounces fresh spinach, washed and chopped
- 1 cup feta cheese, crumbled
- 2 eggs, lightly beaten
- 1/4 cup fresh dill, chopped
- Salt and pepper to taste
- 1/4 teaspoon grated nutmeg

 Prep Time: 20 min

 Cook Time: 40 min

 Serves: 6

DIRECTIONS

Preheat the oven to 350°F (175°C). Lightly oil a 9-inch pie dish.

In a large skillet, heat 1 tablespoon of olive oil over medium heat. Add onion and garlic, and sauté until soft. Add spinach and cook until wilted. Remove from heat and let cool slightly. Stir in feta, eggs, dill, nutmeg, and season with salt and pepper.

Lay one sheet of phyllo in the prepared pie dish, allowing the edges to hang over the sides. Brush lightly with olive oil. Lay another sheet on top, slightly rotated, and brush with oil again. Repeat with four more sheets.

Spread the spinach mixture evenly over the phyllo. Fold the overhanging dough over the filling. Cover the top with the remaining phyllo sheets, brushing each with oil and tucking in the edges to seal.

Bake in the preheated oven until the pie is golden and crisp, about 30-35 minutes. Let cool for 10 minutes before slicing.

Nutritional Information: 330 calories, 9g protein, 23g carbohydrates, 23g fat, 2g fiber, 80mg cholesterol, 560mg sodium, 370mg potassium.

Lebanese Labneh with Olive Tapenade

INGREDIENTS

- 2 cups labneh (strained yogurt)
- 1/2 cup mixed olives, pitted and finely chopped
- 2 tablespoons capers, rinsed and chopped
- 1 clove garlic, minced
- 3 tablespoons olive oil
- 1 tablespoon lemon juice
- 1/4 cup fresh parsley, chopped
- Salt and pepper to taste
- Optional: Warm pita bread for serving

 Prep Time: 15 min

 Cook Time: 0 min

 Serves: 4

DIRECTIONS

In a small bowl, combine the chopped olives, capers, garlic, olive oil, and lemon juice. Mix well to create the olive tapenade.

Spread the labneh in a shallow serving dish. With the back of a spoon, create a well in the center.

Spoon the olive tapenade into the well in the labneh.

Sprinkle the chopped parsley over the top, and season with a pinch of salt and pepper.

Serve immediately with warm pita bread for dipping.

Nutritional Information: 250 calories, 9g protein, 7g carbohydrates, 20g fat, 2g fiber, 10mg cholesterol, 680mg sodium, 190mg potassium.

Turkish Menemen (Scrambled Eggs with Vegetables)

INGREDIENTS

- 6 large eggs
- 2 tablespoons olive oil
- 1 medium onion, diced
- 1 green bell pepper, seeded and diced
- 2 tomatoes, diced
- 1 teaspoon paprika
- 1/2 teaspoon black pepper
- Salt to taste
- Optional: chopped fresh parsley or chives for garnish

 Prep Time: 10 min

 Cook Time: 15 min

 Serves: 4

DIRECTIONS

Heat olive oil in a large skillet over medium heat. Add the onion and bell pepper, and sauté until softened, about 5 minutes.

Add the diced tomatoes and cook until the tomatoes are soft and begin to form a sauce, about 5 more minutes. Stir in paprika, black pepper, and salt.

Crack the eggs directly into the skillet over the vegetable mixture. Let sit for about 1 minute, then gently stir to combine and scramble the eggs with the vegetables. Cook until the eggs are fully set, about 5 minutes.

Remove from heat, garnish with fresh parsley or chives if desired, and serve hot.

Nutritional Information: 220 calories, 13g protein, 8g carbohydrates, 16g fat, 2g fiber, 372mg cholesterol, 190mg sodium, 340mg potassium.

Hummus Rolls with Vegetables

INGREDIENTS

- 4 large whole wheat tortillas
- 1 cup hummus
- 1 red bell pepper, thinly sliced
- 1 cucumber, thinly sliced
- 1 carrot, julienned
- 1/2 cup baby spinach leaves
- 1/4 cup red onion, thinly sliced
- Optional: Fresh parsley or cilantro for garnish

Prep Time:1 5 min

Cook Time: 0 min

Serves: 4

DIRECTIONS

Lay out the tortillas on a flat surface. Spread each tortilla evenly with about 1/4 cup of hummus.

Arrange an even layer of red bell pepper, cucumber, carrot, spinach, and red onion on top of the hummus on each tortilla.

Carefully roll up the tortillas tightly to enclose the filling. If needed, you can use a little extra hummus at the edge to help seal the roll.

Cut each roll into 1-inch pieces if desired, or serve whole. Garnish with fresh parsley or cilantro if using.

Nutritional Information: 320 calories, 12g protein, 45g carbohydrates, 12g fat, 8g fiber, 0mg cholesterol, 580mg sodium, 460mg potassium.

Italian Frittata with Zucchini and Goat Cheese

INGREDIENTS

- 6 large eggs
- 1/4 cup milk
- 1 medium zucchini, thinly sliced
- 1/2 cup crumbled goat cheese
- 2 tablespoons olive oil
- Salt and pepper to taste
- Optional: fresh basil or thyme for garnish

 Prep Time: 10 min

 Cook Time: 15 min

 Serves: 4

DIRECTIONS

In a medium bowl, whisk together eggs, milk, salt, and pepper.

Heat olive oil in an oven-safe skillet over medium heat. Add the sliced zucchini and sauté until tender, about 5 minutes.

Pour the egg mixture over the zucchini in the skillet. Sprinkle the goat cheese evenly on top.

Cook over medium heat until the edges begin to set, about 2-3 minutes. Then transfer the skillet to a preheated 350°F oven.

Bake until the frittata is set and golden, about 10 minutes. Garnish with fresh herbs if desired, and serve.

Nutritional Information: 260 calories, 18g protein, 4g carbohydrates, 20g fat, 1g fiber, 320mg cholesterol, 390mg sodium, 300mg potassium.

Sweet Breakfasts

Greek Yogurt with Honey and Walnuts

INGREDIENTS

- 2 cups Greek yogurt
- 4 tablespoons honey
- 1/2 cup walnuts, chopped
- Optional: fresh berries or sliced fruit for topping

 Prep Time: 5 min

 Cook Time: 0 min

 Serves: 4

DIRECTIONS

Spoon the Greek yogurt into four bowls or serving dishes.

Drizzle each serving with 1 tablespoon of honey.

Sprinkle chopped walnuts evenly over the top of the yogurt.

If desired, add fresh berries or sliced fruit on top for extra flavor and color.

Nutritional Information: 210 calories, 12g protein, 18g carbohydrates, 10g fat, 1g fiber, 10mg cholesterol, 50mg sodium, 200mg potassium.

Date and Nut Porridge

INGREDIENTS

- 1 cup rolled oats
- 4 cups almond milk
- 1/2 cup dates, pitted and chopped
- 1/2 cup mixed nuts (walnuts, almonds, pecans), chopped
- 1 teaspoon cinnamon
- Optional: drizzle of honey or maple syrup for extra sweetness

Prep Time: 5 min

Cook Time: 10 min

Serves: 4

DIRECTIONS

In a medium saucepan, bring the almond milk to a gentle boil. Add the rolled oats and simmer on low heat, stirring occasionally, for about 5 minutes.

Stir in the chopped dates, mixed nuts, and cinnamon. Continue to cook for another 5 minutes or until the oats are soft and the porridge has thickened to your liking.

Remove from heat and let sit for a couple of minutes to cool slightly. The porridge will thicken further as it cools.

Serve warm, with an optional drizzle of honey or maple syrup if a sweeter taste is desired.

Nutritional Information: 340 calories, 10g protein, 50g carbohydrates, 14g fat, 7g fiber, 0mg cholesterol, 100mg sodium, 400mg potassium.

Fig and Honey Toast

INGREDIENTS

- 4 slices of whole-grain bread
- 1/2 cup ricotta cheese
- 4 fresh figs, sliced
- 4 teaspoons honey
- 2 tablespoons chopped walnuts
- Optional: a sprinkle of cinnamon or fresh thyme leaves

Prep Time: 5 min

Cook Time: 5 min

Serves: 4

DIRECTIONS

Toast the whole-grain bread slices to your preferred level of crispiness.

Spread each slice generously with ricotta cheese.

Arrange the sliced figs evenly over the ricotta on each slice of toast.

Drizzle each piece with honey and sprinkle with chopped walnuts.

If desired, add a light sprinkle of cinnamon or a few fresh thyme leaves for additional flavor.

Nutritional Information: 230 calories, 8g protein, 35g carbohydrates, 7g fat, 5g fiber, 15mg cholesterol, 180mg sodium, 240mg potassium.

Pomegranate and Pistachio Müesli

INGREDIENTS

- 2 cups rolled oats
- 1/2 cup pomegranate seeds
- 1/2 cup shelled pistachios, chopped
- 1/4 cup dried cranberries or cherries
- 2 tablespoons chia seeds
- 2 cups almond milk or any milk of choice
- Optional: honey or maple syrup for additional sweetness

Prep Time: 10 min

Cook Time: 0 min

Serves: 4

DIRECTIONS

In a large bowl, combine rolled oats, pomegranate seeds, chopped pistachios, dried cranberries, and chia seeds.

Pour almond milk over the mixture and stir to combine. Let the müesli soak for at least 5 minutes before serving to allow the oats and chia seeds to absorb some of the liquid and soften.

Serve the müesli in bowls, and if a sweeter taste is desired, drizzle with honey or maple syrup.

Nutritional Information: 380 calories, 12g protein, 53g carbohydrates, 15g fat, 9g fiber, 0mg cholesterol, 30mg sodium, 410mg potassium.

Orange and Polenta Cake

INGREDIENTS

- 1 cup polenta (coarse cornmeal)
- 1/2 cup all-purpose flour
- 1 teaspoon baking powder
- 1/2 teaspoon salt
- 3 large eggs
- 3/4 cup granulated sugar
- 1/2 cup olive oil
- Zest of 2 oranges
- Juice of 1 orange (about 1/4 cup)
- Optional: Powdered sugar for dusting

Prep Time: 15 min

Cook Time: 40 min

Serves: 6

DIRECTIONS

Preheat the oven to 350°F (175°C). Grease and line an 8-inch round cake pan with parchment paper.

In a bowl, mix together the polenta, flour, baking powder, and salt.

In another bowl, whisk the eggs and granulated sugar until light and fluffy. Gradually add the olive oil, orange zest, and orange juice, continuing to whisk until well combined.

Fold the dry ingredients into the wet ingredients until just combined. Pour the batter into the prepared cake pan.

Bake in the preheated oven for about 40 minutes, or until a toothpick inserted into the center comes out clean.

Let the cake cool in the pan for 10 minutes, then transfer to a wire rack to cool completely. Dust with powdered sugar before serving if desired.

Nutritional Information: 390 calories, 6g protein, 45g carbohydrates, 21g fat, 2g fiber, 106mg cholesterol, 220mg sodium, 70mg potassium.

Honey-Sweetened Ricotta with Berries

INGREDIENTS

- 2 cups ricotta cheese
- 2 tablespoons honey, plus extra for drizzling
- 1 cup mixed berries (such as blueberries, raspberries, and strawberries)
- Optional: mint leaves for garnish

Prep Time: 5 min

Cook Time: 0 min

Serves: 4

DIRECTIONS

In a mixing bowl, combine the ricotta cheese and 2 tablespoons of honey. Stir until well mixed and smooth.

Spoon the honey-sweetened ricotta into serving bowls.

Top each serving with a generous helping of mixed berries.

Drizzle a little more honey over the berries and ricotta for added sweetness.

Garnish with mint leaves if desired, and serve immediately.

Nutritional Information: 250 calories, 14g protein, 18g carbohydrates, 12g fat, 2g fiber, 50mg cholesterol, 150mg sodium, 120mg potassium.

Berry and Mascarpone Bruschetta

INGREDIENTS

- 4 slices of whole-grain bread
- 1 cup mascarpone cheese
- 1 cup mixed fresh berries (such as strawberries, blueberries, and raspberries)
- 2 tablespoons honey
- Optional: Fresh mint leaves for garnish

Prep Time: 10 min

Cook Time: 5 min

Serves: 4

DIRECTIONS

Toast the slices of whole-grain bread until golden and crispy.

Spread each slice evenly with mascarpone cheese.

Arrange the mixed berries on top of the mascarpone.

Drizzle honey over the berries on each bruschetta.

Garnish with fresh mint leaves if desired, and serve immediately.

Nutritional Information: 330 calories, 8g protein, 32g carbohydrates, 18g fat, 4g fiber, 45mg cholesterol, 150mg sodium, 120mg potassium.

Apricot and Walnut Stuffed Crepes

INGREDIENTS

- 1 cup all-purpose flour
- 2 eggs
- 1 1/2 cups milk
- 1 tablespoon sugar
- Pinch of salt
- 2 tablespoons melted butter, plus extra for cooking
- 1/2 cup apricot preserves
- 1/2 cup chopped walnuts
- Powdered sugar for dusting

Prep Time: 15 min

Cook Time: 20 min

Serves: 4

DIRECTIONS

In a mixing bowl, combine the flour, eggs, milk, sugar, and salt. Whisk until smooth. Stir in the melted butter to form a thin batter.

Heat a small amount of butter in a non-stick skillet over medium heat. Pour about 1/4 cup of batter into the skillet, tilting to spread evenly. Cook until the edges lift and the bottom is lightly browned, about 2 minutes, then flip and cook the other side for 1 minute. Remove and keep warm. Repeat with the remaining batter.

Spread each crepe with a thin layer of apricot preserves, then sprinkle with chopped walnuts.

Roll up the crepes and place them seam-side down on serving plates.

Dust with powdered sugar before serving.

Nutritional Information: 370 calories, 10g protein, 44g carbohydrates, 18g fat, 2g fiber, 115mg cholesterol, 150mg sodium, 200mg potassium.

Cherry and Almond Oatmeal

INGREDIENTS

- 2 cups rolled oats
- 4 cups water or almond milk
- 1 cup fresh or frozen cherries, pitted and halved
- 1/2 cup slivered almonds
- 1/4 cup honey or to taste
- 1 teaspoon vanilla extract
- Optional: a pinch of cinnamon for added flavor

Prep Time: 5 min

Cook Time: 10 min

Serves: 4

DIRECTIONS

In a medium saucepan, bring the water or almond milk to a boil. Add the rolled oats and reduce the heat to a simmer.

Cook the oats, stirring occasionally, until they are soft and have absorbed most of the liquid, about 5 minutes.

Stir in the cherries, slivered almonds, and vanilla extract. Continue to cook for another 2-3 minutes, or until the cherries are warm and slightly softened.

Remove from heat and stir in the honey. Sprinkle with a pinch of cinnamon if using.

Serve warm, with additional honey or almonds on top if desired.

Nutritional Information: 320 calories, 9g protein, 50g carbohydrates, 9g fat, 7g fiber, 0mg cholesterol, 30mg sodium, 200mg potassium.

Greek Salad (Horiatiki)

INGREDIENTS

- 3 medium ripe tomatoes, cut into wedges
- 1 cucumber, peeled and sliced into thick half-moons
- 1 small red onion, thinly sliced
- 1/2 cup Kalamata olives
- 7 ounces feta cheese, cut into thick slices or crumbled
- 1/4 cup extra virgin olive oil
- 2 tablespoons red wine vinegar
- 1 teaspoon dried oregano
- Salt and black pepper to taste

Prep Time: 15 min

Cook Time: 0 min

Serves: 4

DIRECTIONS

In a large bowl, combine the tomato wedges, cucumber slices, and red onion.
Add the Kalamata olives and mix gently.
Place the feta cheese on top of the vegetables. Drizzle with olive oil and red wine vinegar.
Sprinkle dried oregano, salt, and black pepper over the salad.
Serve immediately, allowing the flavors to mingle for a few minutes before enjoying.

Nutritional Information: 280 calories, 7g protein, 12g carbohydrates, 23g fat, 3g fiber, 25mg cholesterol, 420mg sodium, 350mg potassium.

Tabbouleh

INGREDIENTS

- 1/2 cup bulgur wheat
- 1 cup boiling water
- 2 cups fresh parsley, finely chopped
- 1/2 cup fresh mint leaves, finely chopped
- 1 medium tomato, diced
- 1/4 cup green onions, thinly sliced
- 1/4 cup lemon juice
- 1/4 cup extra virgin olive oil
- Salt and pepper to taste

Prep Time: 20 min

Cook Time: 0 min

Serves: 4

DIRECTIONS

Place the bulgur in a large bowl and cover with 1 cup of boiling water. Cover the bowl and let it sit for about 10-15 minutes, or until the water is absorbed and the bulgur is tender.
Fluff the bulgur with a fork and allow it to cool to room temperature.
Add the chopped parsley, mint, tomato, and green onions to the bulgur. Toss to combine.
In a small bowl, whisk together the lemon juice, olive oil, salt, and pepper. Pour this dressing over the salad and mix well to coat all the ingredients.
Let the salad sit for at least 30 minutes before serving to allow the flavors to meld together.

Nutritional Information: 220 calories, 4g protein, 24g carbohydrates, 14g fat, 6g fiber, 0mg cholesterol, 30mg sodium, 340mg potassium.

Fattoush Salad

INGREDIENTS

- 2 small pitas, cut into strips or squares
- 1/4 cup olive oil (for dressing)
- 3 tablespoons lemon juice
- 1 teaspoon sumac
- 1/2 teaspoon salt
- 1/4 teaspoon black pepper
- 1 cucumber, diced
- 2 medium tomatoes, diced
- 1/2 red onion, thinly sliced
- 1/2 cup fresh mint leaves, chopped
- 1 cup parsley leaves, chopped
- 1/2 cup radishes, thinly sliced

Prep Time: 15 min

Cook Time: 5 min (for toasting pita)

Serves: 4

DIRECTIONS

Preheat your oven to 375°F (190°C). Spread the pita strips on a baking sheet and toast in the oven until crispy, about 5 minutes. Set aside to cool.

In a small bowl, whisk together the olive oil, lemon juice, sumac, salt, and pepper to create the dressing.

In a large bowl, combine the cucumber, tomatoes, red onion, mint, parsley, and radishes.

Drizzle the dressing over the salad and toss to coat evenly.

Just before serving, add the toasted pita strips to the salad and toss gently to combine.

Nutritional Information: 210 calories, 3g protein, 25g carbohydrates, 12g fat, 4g fiber, 0mg cholesterol, 310mg sodium, 370mg potassium.

Italian Panzanella

INGREDIENTS

- 4 cups of stale bread, cubed and toasted
- 3 medium ripe tomatoes, cut into chunks
- 1 small red onion, thinly sliced
- 1 cucumber, seeded and sliced
- 20 basil leaves, torn
- 1/4 cup extra virgin olive oil
- 2 tablespoons balsamic vinegar
- Salt and pepper to taste

Prep Time: 20 min

Cook Time: 0 min

Serves: 4

DIRECTIONS

In a large bowl, combine the toasted bread cubes, tomato chunks, sliced red onion, and sliced cucumber.

In a small bowl, whisk together the olive oil, balsamic vinegar, salt, and pepper to create the dressing.

Pour the dressing over the salad ingredients in the large bowl and toss well to combine. Make sure the bread soaks up the dressing.

Let the salad sit for about 15 minutes to allow the flavors to meld and the bread to absorb the dressing fully.

Just before serving, sprinkle the torn basil leaves over the salad and give it one final toss.

Nutritional Information: 290 calories, 6g protein, 35g carbohydrates, 14g fat, 4g fiber, 0mg cholesterol, 340mg sodium, 410mg potassium.

Moroccan Carrot Salad

INGREDIENTS

- 4 cups carrots, peeled and grated
- 1/4 cup olive oil
- 3 tablespoons lemon juice
- 2 cloves garlic, minced
- 1 teaspoon ground cumin
- 1/2 teaspoon salt
- 1/4 teaspoon ground cinnamon
- Optional: 1/4 cup chopped fresh parsley or cilantro for garnish

Prep Time: 15 min

Cook Time: 0 min

Serves: 4

DIRECTIONS

In a large mixing bowl, combine the grated carrots with the minced garlic, ground cumin, salt, and ground cinnamon.

Whisk together the olive oil and lemon juice in a small bowl. Pour this dressing over the carrot mixture and toss thoroughly to ensure all the carrots are evenly coated.

Allow the salad to marinate in the refrigerator for at least 30 minutes to blend the flavors together.

Before serving, toss the salad again and sprinkle with fresh parsley or cilantro if using.

Nutritional Information: 190 calories, 1g protein, 14g carbohydrates, 14g fat, 3g fiber, 0mg cholesterol, 320mg sodium, 360mg potassium.

Caponata Salad

INGREDIENTS

- 1 large eggplant, cubed
- 1 red bell pepper, chopped
- 1 onion, chopped
- 3 tablespoons olive oil
- 2 tablespoons capers, rinsed
- 1/4 cup red wine vinegar
- 1 tablespoon sugar
- 1/4 cup chopped fresh basil
- Salt and pepper to taste

Prep Time: 15 min

Cook Time: 25 min

Serves: 4

DIRECTIONS

Heat the olive oil in a large skillet over medium heat. Add the eggplant, bell pepper, and onion. Cook, stirring occasionally, until the vegetables are softened and golden, about 10 minutes.

Stir in the capers, red wine vinegar, and sugar. Continue to cook for another 15 minutes on low heat, stirring occasionally, until the vegetables are tender and the flavors have melded.

Remove from heat and allow to cool to room temperature.

Stir in the chopped basil, and season with salt and pepper to taste.

Serve the caponata chilled or at room temperature.

Nutritional Information: 180 calories, 2g protein, 20g carbohydrates, 10g fat, 6g fiber, 0mg cholesterol, 320mg sodium, 450mg potassium.

Lebanese Lentil Salad

INGREDIENTS

- 1 cup dried green lentils
- 2 cups water
- 1 cucumber, diced
- 1 red bell pepper, diced
- 1/4 cup chopped fresh parsley
- 1/4 cup olive oil
- 3 tablespoons lemon juice
- Salt and pepper to taste

Prep Time: 10 min

Cook Time: 20 min

Serves: 4

DIRECTIONS

Rinse the lentils under cold water, then place them in a saucepan with 2 cups of water. Bring to a boil, reduce heat, and simmer uncovered until lentils are tender but still firm, about 20 minutes. Drain and let cool.

In a large bowl, combine the cooled lentils, diced cucumber, red bell pepper, and chopped parsley.

In a small bowl, whisk together the olive oil, lemon juice, salt, and pepper to create the dressing.

Pour the dressing over the lentil mixture and toss well to coat. Adjust seasoning as needed.

Serve chilled or at room temperature.

Nutritional Information: 265 calories, 11g protein, 31g carbohydrates, 14g fat, 12g fiber, 0mg cholesterol, 30mg sodium, 410mg potassium.

Mediterranean Chickpea Salad

INGREDIENTS

- 2 cans (15 ounces each) chickpeas, drained and rinsed
- 1 cup cherry tomatoes, halved
- 1 cucumber, diced
- 1/2 red onion, thinly sliced
- 1/4 cup chopped fresh parsley
- 1/4 cup olive oil
- 3 tablespoons lemon juice
- 1 clove garlic, minced
- Salt and pepper to taste

Prep Time: 10 min

Cook Time: 0 min

Serves: 4

DIRECTIONS

In a large bowl, combine the chickpeas, cherry tomatoes, cucumber, red onion, and fresh parsley.

In a small bowl, whisk together the olive oil, lemon juice, minced garlic, salt, and pepper to create the dressing.

Pour the dressing over the salad ingredients and toss well to ensure everything is evenly coated.

Let the salad sit for at least 10 minutes before serving to allow the flavors to meld together.

Serve chilled or at room temperature, perfect as a side dish or a light meal.

Nutritional Information: 340 calories, 12g protein, 45g carbohydrates, 14g fat, 12g fiber, 0mg cholesterol, 300mg sodium, 450mg potassium.

Mediterranean Quinoa Salad

INGREDIENTS

- 1 cup quinoa
- 2 cups water
- 1 cup cherry tomatoes, halved
- 1 cucumber, diced
- 1/2 red onion, finely chopped
- 1/4 cup kalamata olives, pitted and sliced
- 1/4 cup crumbled feta cheese
- 1/4 cup extra virgin olive oil
- 3 tablespoons lemon juice
- Salt and pepper to taste

Prep Time: 10 min

Cook Time: 15 min

Serves: 4

DIRECTIONS

Rinse quinoa under cold water until water runs clear. Combine quinoa and water in a medium saucepan. Bring to a boil, reduce heat to low, cover, and simmer until quinoa is tender and water is absorbed, about 15 minutes. Remove from heat and let sit, covered, for 5 minutes. Fluff with a fork and let cool.

In a large bowl, combine cooled quinoa, cherry tomatoes, cucumber, red onion, kalamata olives, and feta cheese.

In a small bowl, whisk together olive oil, lemon juice, salt, and pepper to create the dressing.

Pour dressing over the quinoa mixture and toss to combine thoroughly.

Refrigerate for at least 30 minutes to allow flavors to meld before serving. Serve chilled or at room temperature.

Nutritional Information: 310 calories, 8g protein, 35g carbohydrates, 16g fat, 5g fiber, 8mg cholesterol, 240mg sodium, 390mg potassium.

Balela Salad

INGREDIENTS

- 1 can (15 oz) chickpeas, drained and rinsed
- 1 can (15 oz) black beans, drained and rinsed
- 1 cup cherry tomatoes, halved
- 1/4 cup finely chopped red onion
- 1/4 cup chopped fresh parsley
- 1/4 cup chopped fresh mint
- 3 tablespoons olive oil
- 2 tablespoons lemon juice
- 1 tablespoon apple cider vinegar
- Salt and pepper to taste

Prep Time: 10 min

Cook Time: 0 min

Serves: 4

DIRECTIONS

In a large bowl, combine chickpeas, black beans, cherry tomatoes, red onion, parsley, and mint.

In a small bowl, whisk together olive oil, lemon juice, and apple cider vinegar to create the dressing.

Pour the dressing over the salad ingredients and toss well to ensure everything is evenly coated.

Season with salt and pepper according to taste.

Chill in the refrigerator for at least 30 minutes before serving to enhance the flavors.

Nutritional Information: 265 calories, 10g protein, 35g carbohydrates, 10g fat, 10g fiber, 0mg cholesterol, 410mg sodium, 450mg potassium.

Watermelon and Feta Salad

INGREDIENTS

- 4 cups cubed watermelon
- 1 cup crumbled feta cheese
- 1/4 cup fresh mint leaves, chopped
- 2 tablespoons balsamic glaze

Prep Time: 10 min

Cook Time: 0 min

Serves: 4

DIRECTIONS

In a large bowl, combine the cubed watermelon and crumbled feta cheese.
Gently toss the watermelon and feta with the chopped mint leaves.
Drizzle the balsamic glaze over the salad just before serving.
Serve immediately or chill in the refrigerator for a refreshing summer dish.

Nutritional Information: 160 calories, 5g protein, 18g carbohydrates, 7g fat, 1g fiber, 25mg cholesterol, 320mg sodium, 170mg potassium.

Artichoke and Roasted Red Pepper Salad

INGREDIENTS

- 1 can (14 oz) artichoke hearts, drained and quartered
- 1 cup roasted red peppers, sliced
- 1/4 cup Kalamata olives, pitted and halved
- 2 tablespoons olive oil
- 1 tablespoon red wine vinegar
- Salt and pepper to taste
- Optional: fresh parsley for garnish

Prep Time: 10 min

Cook Time: 0 min

Serves: 4

DIRECTIONS

In a large mixing bowl, combine the artichoke hearts, sliced roasted red peppers, and Kalamata olives.
Drizzle olive oil and red wine vinegar over the salad. Toss gently to coat all the ingredients evenly.
Season with salt and pepper according to taste.
Chill in the refrigerator for about 30 minutes to allow flavors to meld.
Serve chilled, garnished with fresh parsley if desired.

Nutritional Information: 150 calories, 3g protein, 13g carbohydrates, 10g fat, 5g fiber, 0mg cholesterol, 480mg sodium, 250mg potassium.

Greek Potato Salad

INGREDIENTS

- 1.5 pounds small red potatoes, quartered
- 1/4 cup olive oil
- 3 tablespoons lemon juice
- 1 tablespoon dried oregano
- 1/2 cup red onion, thinly sliced
- 1/2 cup Kalamata olives, pitted and halved
- Salt and pepper to taste
- Optional: fresh parsley, chopped for garnish

Prep Time: 10 min

Cook Time: 20 min

Serves: 4

DIRECTIONS

Place the potatoes in a large pot of salted water. Bring to a boil and cook until tender but still firm, about 15-20 minutes. Drain and let cool slightly.

In a small bowl, whisk together the olive oil, lemon juice, and oregano to create the dressing.

In a large bowl, combine the cooked potatoes, sliced red onion, and Kalamata olives.

Pour the dressing over the potato mixture and gently toss to coat evenly.

Season with salt and pepper to taste. Chill in the refrigerator for at least 30 minutes to allow the flavors to meld.

Serve chilled, garnished with chopped parsley if desired.

Nutritional Information: 250 calories, 3g protein, 28g carbohydrates, 14g fat, 3g fiber, 0mg cholesterol, 200mg sodium, 700mg potassium.

Mediterranean Pasta Salad

INGREDIENTS

- 8 ounces fusilli pasta
- 1/2 cup sun-dried tomatoes, chopped
- 1/2 cup artichoke hearts, chopped
- 1/2 cup Kalamata olives, sliced
- 1/4 cup capers
- 1/4 cup red onion, thinly sliced
- 1/3 cup feta cheese, crumbled
- 1/3 cup extra virgin olive oil
- 3 tablespoons red wine vinegar
- 1 teaspoon dried oregano
- Salt and pepper to taste

Prep Time: 15 min

Cook Time: 10 min

Serves: 4

DIRECTIONS

Cook the pasta according to package instructions until al dente. Drain and rinse under cold water to cool.

In a large bowl, combine the cooked pasta, sun-dried tomatoes, artichoke hearts, Kalamata olives, capers, and red onion.

In a small bowl, whisk together the olive oil, red wine vinegar, oregano, salt, and pepper to create the dressing.

Pour the dressing over the pasta mixture and toss well to ensure everything is evenly coated.

Gently fold in the crumbled feta cheese.

Refrigerate the salad for at least 1 hour before serving to allow the flavors to meld.

Nutritional Information: 410 calories, 10g protein, 45g carbohydrates, 22g fat, 4g fiber, 15mg cholesterol, 530mg sodium, 290mg potassium.

Hummus

INGREDIENTS

- 1 can (15 oz) chickpeas, drained and rinsed
- 1/4 cup tahini (sesame seed paste)
- 1/4 cup lemon juice
- 2 cloves garlic, minced
- 2 tablespoons olive oil
- 1/2 teaspoon salt
- 1/4 teaspoon ground cumin
- 2 to 3 tablespoons water (as needed)
- Optional: Paprika and chopped parsley for garnish

 Prep Time: 10 min

 Cook Time: 0 min

 Serves: 4

DIRECTIONS

In a food processor, combine the chickpeas, tahini, lemon juice, garlic, olive oil, salt, and cumin. Process until the mixture is smooth.

With the processor running, slowly add water one tablespoon at a time until you achieve the desired consistency.

Taste and adjust seasoning if necessary.

Transfer to a serving dish, drizzle with a little more olive oil, and sprinkle with paprika and chopped parsley if desired.

Serve with fresh vegetables or pita bread for dipping.

Nutritional Information: 280 calories, 8g protein, 20g carbohydrates, 20g fat, 6g fiber, 0mg cholesterol, 300mg sodium, 250mg potassium.

Baba Ganoush

INGREDIENTS

- 2 medium eggplants
- 3 tablespoons tahini
- 2 cloves garlic, minced
- 2 tablespoons lemon juice
- 2 tablespoons olive oil
- Salt to taste
- Optional: 1 tablespoon chopped fresh parsley for garnish

 Prep Time: 10 min

Cook Time: 45 min

Serves: 4

DIRECTIONS

Preheat your oven to 400°F (200°C). Pierce the eggplants with a fork several times and place them on a baking sheet. Roast in the oven until the skin is charred and the inside is tender, about 45 minutes. Remove from oven and let cool.

Once the eggplants are cool enough to handle, peel off the skin and place the flesh in a colander to drain any excess liquid for about 10 minutes.

Transfer the eggplant flesh to a food processor. Add tahini, garlic, lemon juice, and olive oil. Process until smooth.

Season with salt to taste and blend again.

Transfer the baba ganoush to a serving bowl, drizzle with a little olive oil, and sprinkle with chopped parsley if using. Serve with pita bread or fresh vegetables.

Nutritional Information: 180 calories, 3g protein, 13g carbohydrates, 14g fat, 6g fiber, 0mg cholesterol, 300mg sodium, 400mg potassium.

Tzatziki

Prep Time: 15 min   Cook Time: 0 min   Serves: 4

INGREDIENTS

- 1 cup Greek yogurt
- 1 medium cucumber, seeded and grated
- 2 cloves garlic, minced
- 2 tablespoons lemon juice
- 2 tablespoons fresh dill, finely chopped
- Salt and pepper to taste
- Optional: 1 tablespoon olive oil for drizzling

DIRECTIONS

Place the grated cucumber in a sieve and press to squeeze out as much excess liquid as possible. Let it drain for about 5 minutes.

In a medium bowl, combine the drained cucumber, Greek yogurt, minced garlic, lemon juice, and chopped dill. Mix until all ingredients are well incorporated.

Season with salt and pepper to taste. Stir well.

Cover and refrigerate for at least 1 hour to allow the flavors to meld together.

Serve chilled with a drizzle of olive oil on top if desired. Tzatziki is perfect as a dip for vegetables, pita bread, or as a condiment for grilled meats.

Nutritional Information: 70 calories, 4g protein, 6g carbohydrates, 4g fat, 0.5g fiber, 10mg cholesterol, 50mg sodium, 150mg potassium.

Stuffed Grape Leaves (Dolma)

Prep Time: 30 min   Cook Time: 60 min   Serves: 6

INGREDIENTS

- 1 jar (16 oz) grape leaves in brine, rinsed and drained
- 1 cup uncooked long-grain rice
- 1/2 cup olive oil
- 1 large onion, finely chopped
- 2 cloves garlic, minced
- 1/4 cup fresh dill, chopped
- 1/4 cup fresh parsley, chopped
- 1 teaspoon dried mint
- Juice of 2 lemons
- Salt and pepper to taste

DIRECTIONS

In a large skillet over medium heat, heat half the olive oil. Add the onion and garlic, cooking until soft and translucent. Add the rice, dill, parsley, mint, and half of the lemon juice. Cook until the rice is partially cooked (about 10 minutes). Season with salt and pepper.

Prepare the grape leaves by carefully unfolding them and cutting off any stems. Place a spoonful of the rice mixture near the base of each leaf. Fold in the sides and roll the leaf tightly over the filling.

Arrange the stuffed leaves seam side down in a large pot. Drizzle the remaining olive oil and lemon juice over the top. Add enough water to half-cover the rolls.

Place a plate on top of the rolls to keep them submerged and bring to a simmer. Cover and let cook for about 50 minutes, or until the rice is fully cooked.

Allow to cool slightly in the pot before serving. Can be served warm or at room temperature.

Nutritional Information: 210 calories, 4g protein, 31g carbohydrates, 8g fat, 4g fiber, 0mg cholesterol, 400mg sodium, 290mg potassium.

Falafel

INGREDIENTS

- 1 cup dried chickpeas (not canned or cooked)
- 1 small onion, roughly chopped
- 2 cloves of garlic, minced
- 1/4 cup fresh parsley, chopped
- 1 teaspoon ground cumin
- 1 teaspoon ground coriander
- 1/2 teaspoon salt
- 1/4 teaspoon black pepper
- 1/4 teaspoon cayenne pepper
- 2 tablespoons flour (or chickpea flour for gluten-free option)
- Vegetable oil for frying

Prep Time: 20 min (plus overnight soaking)

Cook Time: 10 min

Serves: 4 (about 12 balls)

DIRECTIONS

Place dried chickpeas in a large bowl and cover with plenty of cold water. Allow to soak overnight, or for at least 12 hours. They should double in size and soften slightly.

Drain and rinse the soaked chickpeas thoroughly. Combine them in a food processor with onion, garlic, parsley, cumin, coriander, salt, black pepper, and cayenne. Process until mixture is coarse and grainy.

Transfer the mixture to a bowl, add flour, and mix well. Allow it to rest for 15-30 minutes to help binding the ingredients.

Heat about 2 inches of vegetable oil in a deep skillet over medium heat to 350°F (175°C). While oil is heating, form the chickpea mixture into small balls or slightly flattened patties about the size of a golf ball.

Fry the falafel in batches, being careful not to overcrowd the pan, until golden brown and crispy, about 4-5 minutes. Remove with a slotted spoon and drain on paper towels.

Nutritional Information: 330 calories, 9g protein, 35g carbohydrates, 18g fat, 6g fiber, 0mg cholesterol, 300mg sodium, 410mg potassium.

Marinated Olives

INGREDIENTS

- 2 cups mixed olives, drained
- 1/4 cup extra virgin olive oil
- 2 cloves garlic, thinly sliced
- 1 tablespoon fresh rosemary, chopped
- 1 tablespoon fresh thyme, chopped
- Zest of 1 lemon
- 1 teaspoon crushed red pepper flakes

Prep Time: 10 min

Cook Time: 0 min

Serves: 4

DIRECTIONS

In a medium bowl, combine the olives, olive oil, garlic, rosemary, thyme, lemon zest, and red pepper flakes.

Mix thoroughly to ensure the olives are well coated with the oil and herbs.

Cover the bowl and marinate at room temperature for at least 2 hours, or refrigerate overnight for more developed flavors. Stir occasionally to redistribute the flavors.

Serve the olives at room temperature as a snack or as part of an appetizer platter.

Nutritional Information: 180 calories, 1g protein, 5g carbohydrates, 18g fat, 3g fiber, 0mg cholesterol, 800mg sodium, 50mg potassium.

Muhammara

Prep Time: 15 min   Cook Time: 0 min   Serves: 4

INGREDIENTS

- 1 cup roasted red peppers, drained
- 1/2 cup walnuts, toasted
- 1/4 cup breadcrumbs
- 2 tablespoons olive oil
- 1 tablespoon pomegranate molasses
- 1 teaspoon ground cumin
- 1/2 teaspoon smoked paprika
- 1 clove garlic, minced
- Salt to taste

DIRECTIONS

Place the roasted red peppers, toasted walnuts, breadcrumbs, olive oil, pomegranate molasses, cumin, smoked paprika, and garlic in the bowl of a food processor.

Process until the mixture becomes smooth and well combined. If the mixture is too thick, add a little more olive oil or water to reach a creamy consistency.

Taste and adjust seasoning with salt and additional spices if needed.

Transfer the muhammara to a serving bowl. Cover and let sit for at least 30 minutes to allow the flavors to meld together.

Serve with pita bread, crackers, or as a spread on sandwiches.

Nutritional Information: 210 calories, 3g protein, 12g carbohydrates, 17g fat, 3g fiber, 0mg cholesterol, 200mg sodium, 150mg potassium.

Roasted Chickpeas

Prep Time: 5 min   Cook Time: 30 min   Serves: 4

INGREDIENTS

- 1 can (15 oz) chickpeas, drained, rinsed, and patted dry
- 1 tablespoon olive oil
- 1/2 teaspoon salt
- 1/2 teaspoon ground cumin
- 1/4 teaspoon chili powder

DIRECTIONS

Preheat your oven to 400°F (200°C).

In a bowl, toss the chickpeas with olive oil, salt, cumin, and chili powder until evenly coated.

Spread the chickpeas in a single layer on a baking sheet.

Roast in the preheated oven for about 30 minutes, stirring every 10 minutes, until the chickpeas are golden and crispy.

Remove from the oven and let cool on the baking sheet. They will continue to crisp as they cool.

Nutritional Information: 150 calories, 6g protein, 20g carbohydrates, 5g fat, 6g fiber, 0mg cholesterol, 300mg sodium, 210mg potassium.

Fried Calamari

INGREDIENTS

- 1 pound calamari, cleaned and sliced into rings
- 1 cup all-purpose flour
- 1 teaspoon salt
- 1/2 teaspoon black pepper
- Vegetable oil for frying
- Lemon wedges for serving

Prep Time: 10 min

Cook Time: 5 min

Serves: 4

DIRECTIONS

In a large bowl, combine flour, salt, and pepper.

Toss the calamari rings in the flour mixture until they are well coated.

Heat oil in a deep fryer or large skillet to 375°F (190°C).

Fry the calamari in batches, being careful not to overcrowd the fryer, until golden and crispy, about 2-3 minutes.

Remove the calamari with a slotted spoon and drain on paper towels. Serve hot with lemon wedges.

Nutritional Information: 280 calories, 18g protein, 20g carbohydrates, 12g fat, 1g fiber, 175mg cholesterol, 480mg sodium, 300mg potassium.

Artichoke Hearts with Vinaigrette

INGREDIENTS

- 1 can (14 ounces) artichoke hearts, drained and halved
- 1/4 cup extra virgin olive oil
- 2 tablespoons red wine vinegar
- 1 clove garlic, minced
- 1 teaspoon dried oregano
- Salt and pepper to taste

Prep Time: 10 min

Cook Time: 0 min

Serves: 4

DIRECTIONS

In a medium bowl, whisk together the olive oil, red wine vinegar, minced garlic, dried oregano, salt, and pepper to create the vinaigrette.

Add the drained and halved artichoke hearts to the bowl with the vinaigrette. Toss gently to coat the artichokes thoroughly.

Let the artichoke hearts marinate in the vinaigrette for at least 30 minutes at room temperature, or cover and refrigerate for up to 24 hours for more developed flavors.

Serve the marinated artichoke hearts as part of an appetizer platter or as a side dish.

Nutritional Information: 190 calories, 2g protein, 8g carbohydrates, 16g fat, 4g fiber, 0mg cholesterol, 360mg sodium, 240mg potassium.

Saganaki (Fried Cheese)

INGREDIENTS

- 8 ounces Kasseri, Kefalotyri, or Halloumi cheese, sliced into 1/2-inch thick pieces
- 1/4 cup all-purpose flour
- 2 tablespoons olive oil
- Lemon wedges for serving

 Prep Time: 5 min

 Cook Time: 5 min

 Serves: 4

DIRECTIONS

Lightly dust the cheese slices with flour, shaking off any excess.
Heat the olive oil in a medium frying pan over medium-high heat.
Once the oil is hot, add the cheese slices to the pan. Fry for about 2 minutes on each side or until the cheese is golden brown and has started to melt slightly.
Remove the cheese from the pan and immediately squeeze lemon juice over the top.
Serve hot, accompanied by additional lemon wedges.

Nutritional Information: 300 calories, 18g protein, 6g carbohydrates, 24g fat, 0g fiber, 50mg cholesterol, 800mg sodium, 30mg potassium.

Mediterranean Shrimp Antipasto

INGREDIENTS

- 1 pound large shrimp, peeled and deveined
- 2 tablespoons olive oil
- 2 cloves garlic, minced
- 1 teaspoon dried oregano
- 1/2 teaspoon red pepper flakes
- Salt and pepper to taste
- Lemon wedges for serving

 Prep Time: 10 min

 Cook Time: 5 min

 Serves: 4

DIRECTIONS

Heat the olive oil in a large skillet over medium-high heat.
Add the minced garlic and red pepper flakes to the skillet and sauté for about 1 minute, until fragrant.
Add the shrimp to the skillet, sprinkle with dried oregano, salt, and pepper, and cook for about 2-3 minutes on each side or until the shrimp are pink and opaque.
Remove from heat and transfer to a serving platter. Serve hot with lemon wedges on the side for squeezing over the shrimp.

Nutritional Information: 180 calories, 23g protein, 1g carbohydrates, 10g fat, 0g fiber, 180mg cholesterol, 300mg sodium, 200mg potassium.

Mediterranean Stuffed Peppers

INGREDIENTS

- 4 large bell peppers, tops cut off and seeds removed
- 1 cup cooked quinoa
- 1 can (15 oz) chickpeas, drained and rinsed
- 1 cup chopped spinach
- 1/2 cup crumbled feta cheese
- 1/4 cup chopped kalamata olives
- 2 cloves garlic, minced
- 2 tablespoons olive oil
- 1 teaspoon dried oregano
- Salt and pepper to taste

Prep Time: 20 min

Cook Time: 30 min

Serves: 4

DIRECTIONS

Preheat the oven to 375°F (190°C). Arrange the bell peppers in a baking dish with the cut sides up.

In a large bowl, mix together the cooked quinoa, chickpeas, chopped spinach, crumbled feta, kalamata olives, minced garlic, olive oil, dried oregano, salt, and pepper.

Spoon the quinoa mixture into each bell pepper until well filled.

Cover the baking dish with aluminum foil and bake in the preheated oven for about 25 minutes.

Remove the foil and continue baking for an additional 5 minutes or until the peppers are tender and the filling is heated through.

Nutritional Information: 290 calories, 9g protein, 34g carbohydrates, 14g fat, 7g fiber, 15mg cholesterol, 420mg sodium, 530mg potassium.

Tapenade

INGREDIENTS

- 1 cup pitted Kalamata olives
- 2 tablespoons capers, rinsed and drained
- 2 anchovy fillets, rinsed (optional)
- 1 clove garlic, minced
- 1/4 cup olive oil
- 1 tablespoon lemon juice
- 1 teaspoon fresh thyme leaves

Prep Time: 10 min

Cook Time: 0 min

Serves: 4

DIRECTIONS

In the bowl of a food processor, combine the Kalamata olives, capers, anchovy fillets (if using), minced garlic, and fresh thyme leaves.

Pulse a few times to chop and blend the ingredients. Be careful not to overprocess; the mixture should still have some texture.

With the processor running, slowly add the olive oil and lemon juice until the mixture becomes a coarse paste.

Taste and adjust seasoning if necessary, though additional salt is usually not needed due to the saltiness of the olives and capers.

Transfer the tapenade to a serving bowl and use as a spread on crusty bread, crackers, or as a condiment with grilled meats.

Nutritional Information: 180 calories, 1g protein, 4g carbohydrates, 18g fat, 2g fiber, 2mg cholesterol, 900mg sodium, 50mg potassium.

Flavorful Salad Dressings

Classic Greek Vinaigrette

INGREDIENTS

- 1/2 cup extra virgin olive oil
- 1/4 cup red wine vinegar
- 2 tablespoons lemon juice
- 2 cloves garlic, minced
- 1 teaspoon dried oregano
- Salt and pepper to taste

 Prep Time: 5 min

 Cook Time: 0 min

 Serves: 4

DIRECTIONS

In a small bowl or a jar with a tight-fitting lid, combine the olive oil, red wine vinegar, lemon juice, minced garlic, and dried oregano.

Whisk together the ingredients in the bowl or if using a jar, secure the lid and shake vigorously until all ingredients are well blended.

Season the vinaigrette with salt and pepper to taste. Adjust the seasoning as necessary, adding more lemon juice or vinegar for acidity or more oil for smoothness.

Serve immediately over a Greek salad or store in the refrigerator for up to a week. Shake well before each use.

Nutritional Information: 250 calories, 0g protein, 2g carbohydrates, 27g fat, 0g fiber, 0mg cholesterol, 150mg sodium, 10mg potassium.

Lemon Tahini Dressing

INGREDIENTS

- 1/2 cup tahini
- 1/4 cup lemon juice
- 1 clove garlic, minced
- 1/4 teaspoon salt
- 2 to 4 tablespoons water (as needed to achieve desired consistency)

 Prep Time: 5 min

 Cook Time: 0 min

 Serves: 4

DIRECTIONS

In a medium bowl, combine the tahini, lemon juice, minced garlic, and salt.

Whisk the ingredients together until well blended. The mixture might thicken and seize up initially.

Gradually add water, one tablespoon at a time, whisking continuously until the dressing reaches your preferred consistency. It should be creamy and pourable.

Taste and adjust the seasoning, adding more salt or lemon juice if needed.

Serve immediately, or store in the refrigerator in an airtight container for up to one week. Stir or shake well before using if separated.

Nutritional Information: 190 calories, 6g protein, 8g carbohydrates, 16g fat, 3g fiber, 0mg cholesterol, 150mg sodium, 180mg potassium.

Italian Herb Vinaigrette

INGREDIENTS

- 1/2 cup extra virgin olive oil
- 1/4 cup white wine vinegar
- 1 tablespoon fresh lemon juice
- 1 teaspoon dried Italian seasoning (a blend of oregano, basil, thyme, and rosemary)
- 1 clove garlic, minced
- 1/2 teaspoon dijon mustard
- Salt and pepper to taste

 Prep Time: 5 min

 Cook Time: 0 min

 Serves: 4

DIRECTIONS

In a small bowl or a jar with a tight-fitting lid, combine the olive oil, white wine vinegar, lemon juice, dried Italian seasoning, minced garlic, and dijon mustard.

Whisk together in the bowl or seal the jar and shake vigorously until all ingredients are well blended and the dressing is emulsified.

Season with salt and pepper to taste, adjusting the seasoning as necessary to balance the acidity and flavors.

Serve immediately over your favorite salad or store in the refrigerator for up to a week. Shake well before each use to re-emulsify the ingredients.

Nutritional Information: 250 calories, 0g protein, 1g carbohydrates, 27g fat, 0g fiber, 0mg cholesterol, 150mg sodium, 10mg potassium.

Garlic and Lemon Yogurt Dressing

INGREDIENTS

- 1 cup plain Greek yogurt
- 2 cloves garlic, minced
- 2 tablespoons lemon juice
- 1 tablespoon olive oil
- Salt and pepper to taste

 Prep Time: 5 min

 Cook Time: 0 min

 Serves: 4

DIRECTIONS

In a small bowl, combine the Greek yogurt, minced garlic, lemon juice, and olive oil.

Whisk the ingredients together until smooth and well blended.

Season with salt and pepper to taste. Adjust the lemon juice or garlic according to your preference for more tanginess or a stronger garlic flavor.

Let the dressing chill in the refrigerator for at least 30 minutes before serving to allow the flavors to meld.

Serve over salads, grilled vegetables, or use as a dip for fresh veggies or pita chips.

Nutritional Information: 90 calories, 5g protein, 4g carbohydrates, 6g fat, 0g fiber, 5mg cholesterol, 50mg sodium, 100mg potassium.

Mint and Yogurt Dressing

INGREDIENTS

- 1 cup plain Greek yogurt
- 1/4 cup fresh mint leaves, finely chopped
- 2 tablespoons lemon juice
- 1 clove garlic, minced
- Salt and pepper to taste

Prep Time: 5 min

Cook Time: 0 min

Serves: 4

DIRECTIONS

In a medium bowl, combine the Greek yogurt, chopped mint leaves, lemon juice, and minced garlic.

Stir all the ingredients together until thoroughly blended.

Season with salt and pepper to taste, adjusting the flavors as needed to balance the tanginess and the freshness of the mint.

Refrigerate the dressing for at least 30 minutes before serving to allow the flavors to meld together.

Serve the dressing over fresh salads, with grilled meats, or as a cooling dip for spicy dishes.

Nutritional Information: 60 calories, 5g protein, 4g carbohydrates, 2g fat, 0g fiber, 3mg cholesterol, 45mg sodium, 150mg potassium.

Olive and Caper Vinaigrette

INGREDIENTS

- 1/3 cup extra virgin olive oil
- 3 tablespoons red wine vinegar
- 1/4 cup chopped Kalamata olives
- 2 tablespoons capers, rinsed and chopped
- 1 clove garlic, minced
- Salt and pepper to taste

Prep Time: 10 min

Cook Time: 0 min

Serves: 4

DIRECTIONS

In a small bowl, whisk together the olive oil and red wine vinegar until well blended.

Stir in the chopped olives, capers, and minced garlic.

Season with salt and pepper to taste, keeping in mind that olives and capers already contribute a salty flavor.

Let the dressing sit for at least 10 minutes to allow the flavors to meld together before serving.

Drizzle over fresh greens, roasted vegetables, or use as a marinade for fish or poultry.

Nutritional Information: 180 calories, 0g protein, 2g carbohydrates, 18g fat, 0g fiber, 0mg cholesterol, 380mg sodium, 5mg potassium.

Red Pepper and Almond Dressing

INGREDIENTS

- 1 roasted red pepper, peeled and seeded
- 1/4 cup raw almonds
- 2 tablespoons red wine vinegar
- 1/4 cup extra virgin olive oil
- 1 clove garlic
- Salt and pepper to taste

Prep Time: 10 min   Cook Time: 0 min   Serves: 4

DIRECTIONS

Place the roasted red pepper, almonds, red wine vinegar, and garlic in a blender or food processor.

Blend on high until the mixture is smooth.

With the blender running, slowly drizzle in the olive oil until the dressing is emulsified and creamy.

Season with salt and pepper to taste.

Let the dressing sit for a few minutes to allow the flavors to meld together before serving over salads, grilled vegetables, or as a sauce for chicken or fish.

Nutritional Information: 220 calories, 3g protein, 4g carbohydrates, 22g fat, 2g fiber, 0mg cholesterol, 150mg sodium, 50mg potassium.

Herb and Garlic Vinaigrette

INGREDIENTS

- 1/4 cup extra virgin olive oil
- 2 tablespoons red wine vinegar
- 1 tablespoon fresh lemon juice
- 2 cloves garlic, minced
- 1 tablespoon fresh parsley, finely chopped
- 1 teaspoon fresh thyme leaves
- 1 teaspoon fresh oregano leaves
- Salt and pepper to taste

Prep Time: 5 min   Cook Time: 0 min   Serves: 4

DIRECTIONS

In a small bowl, whisk together the olive oil, red wine vinegar, and lemon juice until well combined.

Stir in the minced garlic, chopped parsley, thyme leaves, and oregano leaves.

Season the vinaigrette with salt and pepper to taste.

Taste and adjust the seasoning, adding more salt, pepper, or lemon juice if desired.

Serve immediately over salads, grilled vegetables, or as a marinade for chicken or fish.

Nutritional Information: 140 calories, 0g protein, 2g carbohydrates, 15g fat, 0g fiber, 0mg cholesterol, 120mg sodium, 30mg potassium.

Orange and Mustard Dressing

Prep Time: 5 min   Cook Time: 0 min   Serves: 4

INGREDIENTS

- 1/4 cup extra virgin olive oil
- 2 tablespoons fresh orange juice
- 1 tablespoon Dijon mustard
- 1 tablespoon honey
- 1 teaspoon orange zest
- Salt and pepper to taste

DIRECTIONS

In a small bowl, whisk together the olive oil, fresh orange juice, Dijon mustard, and honey until well combined.

Stir in the orange zest until evenly distributed.

Season the dressing with salt and pepper to taste.

Taste and adjust the seasoning, adding more salt, pepper, or honey if desired.

Serve immediately over salads, grilled chicken, or roasted vegetables.

Nutritional Information: 130 calories, 0g protein, 6g carbohydrates, 12g fat, 0g fiber, 0mg cholesterol, 120mg sodium, 20mg potassium.

Sundried Tomato Dressing

Prep Time: 10 min   Cook Time: 0 min   Serves: 4

INGREDIENTS

- 1/4 cup sundried tomatoes (packed in oil), drained
- 2 tablespoons balsamic vinegar
- 2 tablespoons extra virgin olive oil
- 1 garlic clove, minced
- 1 teaspoon Dijon mustard
- Salt and pepper to taste

DIRECTIONS

In a food processor or blender, combine the sundried tomatoes, balsamic vinegar, olive oil, minced garlic, and Dijon mustard.

Blend until smooth and well combined, scraping down the sides as needed.

Season the dressing with salt and pepper to taste, adjusting as necessary.

If the dressing is too thick, add a splash of water to reach your desired consistency.

Transfer the dressing to a jar or container with a tight-fitting lid and refrigerate until ready to use.

Nutritional Information: 110 calories, 1g protein, 7g carbohydrates, 9g fat, 1g fiber, 0mg cholesterol, 200mg sodium, 120mg potassium.

Lemon and Dill Vinaigrette

INGREDIENTS

- 1/4 cup extra virgin olive oil
- 2 tablespoons fresh lemon juice
- 1 tablespoon chopped fresh dill
- 1 teaspoon Dijon mustard
- 1 small garlic clove, minced
- Salt and pepper to taste

Prep Time: 5 min

Cook Time: 0 min

Serves: 4

DIRECTIONS

In a small bowl, whisk together the olive oil, lemon juice, chopped dill, Dijon mustard, and minced garlic until well combined.

Season the vinaigrette with salt and pepper to taste, adjusting as needed.

Taste and adjust the flavors by adding more lemon juice, dill, mustard, or seasoning, according to your preference.

Serve immediately over your favorite salad or refrigerate in an airtight container until ready to use.

Nutritional Information: 120 calories, 0g protein, 1g carbohydrates, 14g fat, 0g fiber, 0mg cholesterol, 50mg sodium, 10mg potassium.

Chili Lime Dressing

INGREDIENTS

- 1/4 cup olive oil
- 2 tablespoons fresh lime juice
- 1 teaspoon honey
- 1 teaspoon chili powder
- 1/2 teaspoon ground cumin
- 1/4 teaspoon garlic powder
- Salt and pepper to taste

Prep Time: 5 min

Cook Time: 0 min

Serves: 4

DIRECTIONS

In a small bowl, whisk together the olive oil, fresh lime juice, honey, chili powder, ground cumin, and garlic powder until well combined.

Season the dressing with salt and pepper to taste, adjusting as needed.

Taste and adjust the flavors by adding more lime juice, honey, chili powder, or seasoning, according to your preference.

Serve immediately over your favorite salad or refrigerate in an airtight container until ready to use.

Nutritional Information: 120 calories, 0g protein, 3g carbohydrates, 14g fat, 0g fiber, 0mg cholesterol, 50mg sodium, 10mg potassium.

Anchovy Vinaigrette

INGREDIENTS

- 3 anchovy fillets, minced
- 1 garlic clove, minced
- 2 tablespoons red wine vinegar
- 1/4 cup extra virgin olive oil
- Salt and pepper to taste

 Prep Time: 5 min

 Cook Time: 0 min

 Serves: 4

DIRECTIONS

In a small bowl, combine the minced anchovy fillets and minced garlic clove.
Add the red wine vinegar to the bowl and whisk until well combined.
Slowly drizzle in the extra virgin olive oil while whisking continuously until emulsified.
Season the vinaigrette with salt and pepper to taste, adjusting as needed.
Taste and adjust the flavors by adding more vinegar, olive oil, or seasoning, according to your preference.

Nutritional Information: 120 calories, 1g protein, 1g carbohydrates, 14g fat, 0g fiber, 5mg cholesterol, 180mg sodium, 10mg potassium.

Fig and Balsamic Dressing

INGREDIENTS

- 4 fresh figs, stemmed and quartered
- 2 tablespoons balsamic vinegar
- 2 tablespoons extra virgin olive oil
- 1 teaspoon honey
- Salt and pepper to taste

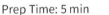 Prep Time: 5 min

 Cook Time: 0 min

 Serves: 4

DIRECTIONS

In a blender or food processor, combine the fresh figs, balsamic vinegar, extra virgin olive oil, and honey.
Blend until smooth and well combined.
If the dressing is too thick, you can add a little water to thin it out to your desired consistency.
Season the dressing with salt and pepper to taste, adjusting as needed.
Transfer the dressing to a jar or container with a tight-fitting lid and store in the refrigerator until ready to use.

Nutritional Information: 80 calories, 1g protein, 10g carbohydrates, 5g fat, 2g fiber, 0mg cholesterol, 60mg sodium, 100mg potassium.

Cilantro and Lime Vinaigrette

INGREDIENTS

- 1/2 cup fresh cilantro leaves, packed
- 1/4 cup lime juice (about 2-3 limes)
- 1/4 cup extra virgin olive oil
- 1 garlic clove, minced
- 1 teaspoon honey
- Salt and pepper to taste

Prep Time: 5 min

Cook Time: 0 min

Serves: 4

DIRECTIONS

In a blender or food processor, combine the fresh cilantro leaves, lime juice, extra virgin olive oil, minced garlic, and honey.

Blend until smooth and well combined.

If the dressing is too thick, you can add a little water to thin it out to your desired consistency.

Season the dressing with salt and pepper to taste, adjusting as needed.

Transfer the dressing to a jar or container with a tight-fitting lid and store in the refrigerator until ready to use.

Nutritional Information: 120 calories, 0g protein, 3g carbohydrates, 13g fat, 0g fiber, 0mg cholesterol, 0mg sodium, 20mg potassium.

Saffron and Orange Dressing

INGREDIENTS

- 1/4 teaspoon saffron threads
- 1/4 cup fresh orange juice (about 1-2 oranges)
- 1/4 cup extra virgin olive oil
- 1 tablespoon honey
- 1 teaspoon Dijon mustard
- Salt and pepper to taste

Prep Time: 5 min

Cook Time: 0 min

Serves: 4

DIRECTIONS

In a small bowl, crush the saffron threads with the back of a spoon to release their flavor.

Add the fresh orange juice to the bowl with the crushed saffron threads and let it sit for a few minutes to infuse.

In a separate bowl, whisk together the infused orange juice and saffron mixture, extra virgin olive oil, honey, and Dijon mustard until well combined.

Season the dressing with salt and pepper to taste, adjusting as needed.

Transfer the dressing to a jar or container with a tight-fitting lid and store in the refrigerator until ready to use.

Nutritional Information: 140 calories, 0g protein, 7g carbohydrates, 14g fat, 0g fiber, 0mg cholesterol, 50mg sodium, 20mg potassium.

Soups

Greek Lemon Chicken Soup (Avgolemono)

INGREDIENTS

- 4 cups chicken broth
- 1 cup water
- 1/2 cup long grain white rice
- 1 cup cooked, shredded chicken
- 3 large eggs
- 2 lemons, juiced (about 1/3 cup)
- Salt and pepper to taste
- Fresh dill or parsley, for garnish (optional)

Prep Time: 20 min

Cook Time: 30 min

Serves: 4

DIRECTIONS

In a large saucepan, bring the chicken broth and water to a boil. Add the rice and simmer until it is tender, about 15 to 20 minutes.

In a separate bowl, whisk the eggs until frothy. Gradually whisk in the lemon juice. Temper the egg mixture by slowly whisking in a cup of the hot broth from the saucepan. This step prevents the eggs from curdling when added to the soup.

Slowly stir the tempered egg mixture back into the saucepan. Add the cooked chicken. Heat the soup gently, without boiling, until it thickens slightly and is just warm enough to serve, about 5 to 7 minutes.

Season with salt and pepper. Serve garnished with fresh dill or parsley if desired.

Nutritional Information: 234 calories, 20g protein, 15g carbohydrates, 10g fat, 1g fiber, 186mg cholesterol, 570mg sodium, 369mg potassium.

Turkish Yogurt Soup (Yayla Çorbası)

INGREDIENTS

- 1 cup rice
- 4 cups chicken or vegetable broth
- 2 cups plain yogurt
- 1 egg
- 2 tablespoons all-purpose flour
- 2 tablespoons butter
- 1 teaspoon dried mint
- Salt and pepper to taste

Prep Time: 15 min

Cook Time: 30 min

Serves: 4

DIRECTIONS

Cook the rice in the broth over medium heat until tender, about 20 minutes.

In a bowl, whisk together the yogurt, egg, and flour until smooth.

Temper the yogurt mixture by slowly whisking in a cup of the hot broth, then gradually stir the tempered yogurt mixture back into the pot.

Reduce the heat to low and cook, stirring constantly, until the soup thickens slightly, about 10 minutes. Be careful not to let the soup boil.

In a small skillet, melt the butter and stir in the dried mint, cooking for a few seconds. Stir the mint butter into the soup. Season with salt and pepper to taste.

Nutritional Information: 290 calories, 13g protein, 34g carbohydrates, 12g fat, 1g fiber, 75mg cholesterol, 300mg sodium, 200mg potassium.

Italian Minestrone Soup

INGREDIENTS

- 2 tablespoons olive oil
- 1 medium onion, diced
- 2 stalks celery, chopped
- 2 carrots, diced
- 3 cloves garlic, minced
- 1 zucchini, diced
- 1 small yellow squash, diced
- 1 cup green beans, trimmed and cut into 1-inch pieces
- 1 can diced tomatoes
- 1 can cannellini beans
- 6 cups vegetable broth
- 1 teaspoon dried oregano
- 1 teaspoon dried basil
- Salt and pepper to taste
- 1 cup small pasta (shells)
- 1/4 cup chopped parsley
- Grated Parmesan cheese

 Prep Time: 20 min

 Cook Time: 40 min

 Serves: 6

DIRECTIONS

Heat the olive oil in a large pot over medium heat. Add onion, celery, carrots, and garlic, sautéing until the vegetables are softened, about 5 minutes.

Add zucchini, yellow squash, green beans, diced tomatoes, cannellini beans, vegetable broth, oregano, and basil. Season with salt and pepper. Bring to a boil, then reduce heat and simmer for 30 minutes.

Stir in the pasta and cook until tender, about 10 minutes. Adjust seasoning as needed.

Serve hot, sprinkled with fresh parsley and grated Parmesan cheese.

Nutritional Information: 235 calories, 12g protein, 42g carbohydrates, 4g fat, 10g fiber, 0mg cholesterol, 690mg sodium, 635mg potassium.

Spanish Gazpacho

INGREDIENTS

- 1 pound ripe tomatoes, roughly chopped
- 1 cucumber, peeled, seeded, and chopped
- 1 bell pepper, seeded and chopped
- 1 small red onion, chopped
- 2 cloves garlic, minced
- 2 tablespoons red wine vinegar
- 1/4 cup extra virgin olive oil
- Salt and pepper to taste
- 1/2 cup cold water (optional, for desired consistency)

 Prep Time: 15 min

 Cook Time: 0 min

 Serves: 4

DIRECTIONS

In a blender or food processor, combine tomatoes, cucumber, bell pepper, red onion, garlic, red wine vinegar, and olive oil.

Blend until the mixture is smooth. If the gazpacho is thicker than preferred, gradually add cold water to reach the desired consistency.

Season with salt and pepper to taste. Chill the gazpacho in the refrigerator for at least 2 hours before serving to enhance the flavors.

Serve cold, optionally garnished with additional chopped cucumber, bell pepper, or a drizzle of olive oil.

Nutritional Information: 180 calories, 2g protein, 15g carbohydrates, 14g fat, 4g fiber, 0mg cholesterol, 12mg sodium, 430mg potassium.

Turkish Red Lentil Soup (Mercimek Çorbası)

INGREDIENTS

- 1 cup red lentils, rinsed
- 1 large onion, finely chopped
- 2 carrots, peeled and diced
- 2 cloves garlic, minced
- 1 tablespoon tomato paste
- 1 teaspoon ground cumin
- 1/2 teaspoon smoked paprika
- 4 cups vegetable broth
- 2 tablespoons olive oil
- Salt and freshly ground black pepper to taste
- Lemon wedges, for serving
- Fresh parsley, chopped, for garnish

Prep Time: 10 min

Cook Time: 25 min

Serves: 4

DIRECTIONS

Heat olive oil in a large pot over medium heat. Add onion, carrots, and garlic, and cook until the onions are translucent and the carrots start to soften, about 5 minutes.

Stir in tomato paste, cumin, and paprika, cooking for 1 minute until fragrant.

Add red lentils and vegetable broth. Bring to a boil, then reduce heat and simmer until lentils are tender, about 20 minutes.

Puree the soup using an immersion blender until smooth. Season with salt and pepper.

Serve hot, garnished with fresh parsley and lemon wedges.

Nutritional Information: 295 calories, 16g protein, 40g carbohydrates, 7g fat, 8g fiber, 0mg cholesterol, 705mg sodium, 540mg potassium.

Greek Chickpea Soup (Revithia)

INGREDIENTS

- 1 cup dried chickpeas, soaked overnight and drained
- 1 large onion, chopped
- 2 cloves garlic, minced
- 1 carrot, diced
- 1 celery stalk, diced
- 1/4 cup olive oil
- 6 cups water
- 1 teaspoon dried oregano
- Salt and pepper to taste
- Lemon wedges, for serving
- Fresh parsley, chopped, for garnish

Prep Time: 10 min (plus overnight soaking)

Cook Time: 90 min

Serves: 4

DIRECTIONS

In a large pot, heat olive oil over medium heat. Add onion, garlic, carrot, and celery, and sauté until the onions are translucent, about 5 minutes.

Add the soaked and drained chickpeas, water, and oregano. Bring to a boil, then reduce the heat to low, cover, and simmer for about 1.5 hours, or until the chickpeas are tender.

Season the soup with salt and pepper to taste. Continue to simmer for a few more minutes to blend the flavors.

Serve hot, garnished with fresh parsley and accompanied by lemon wedges.

Nutritional Information: 290 calories, 10g protein, 35g carbohydrates, 14g fat, 10g fiber, 0mg cholesterol, 240mg sodium, 480mg potassium.

Moroccan Harira Soup

INGREDIENTS

- 1 tablespoon olive oil
- 1 large onion, chopped
- 2 celery stalks, diced
- 2 carrots, diced
- 2 garlic cloves, minced
- 1 pound lamb
- 1 teaspoon ground turmeric
- 1 teaspoon cinnamon
- 1/2 teaspoon ground ginger
- 1/2 teaspoon black pepper
- 1 can diced tomatoes
- 4 cups beef broth
- 1 cup lentils, rinsed
- 1/2 cup chopped cilantro
- 1/2 cup chopped parsley
- 1/4 cup long-grain rice
- Salt to taste
- Lemon wedges, for serving

 Prep Time: 20 min

 Cook Time: 45 min

Serves: 6

DIRECTIONS

Cut the lamb into small cubes.

Heat olive oil in a large pot over medium heat. Add onion, celery, carrots, and garlic. Cook until vegetables are softened, about 5 minutes.

Add lamb, turmeric, cinnamon, ginger, and black pepper. Cook until lamb is browned on all sides, about 10 minutes.

Stir in diced tomatoes, beef broth, and lentils. Bring to a boil, then reduce heat and simmer for 30 minutes, or until lentils are tender.

Add rice, cilantro, and parsley. Cook for an additional 15 minutes, or until rice is cooked. Season with salt to taste.

Serve hot, with lemon wedges on the side for squeezing.

Nutritional Information: 335 calories, 23g protein, 35g carbohydrates, 12g fat, 10g fiber, 45mg cholesterol, 710mg sodium, 790mg potassium.

Greek Tomato and Orzo Soup

INGREDIENTS

- 1 tablespoon olive oil
- 1 small onion, diced
- 2 cloves garlic, minced
- 1 can (28 ounces) crushed tomatoes
- 4 cups vegetable broth
- 1/2 cup orzo pasta
- 1 teaspoon dried oregano
- 1 teaspoon dried basil
- Salt and pepper to taste
- Fresh basil or parsley, chopped, for garnish
- Grated Parmesan cheese, optional, for serving

 Prep Time: 10 min

 Cook Time: 30 min

Serves: 4

DIRECTIONS

Heat olive oil in a large pot over medium heat. Add onion and garlic, and sauté until onion is translucent, about 5 minutes.

Add crushed tomatoes, vegetable broth, oregano, and basil. Bring to a boil.

Reduce heat and simmer for 20 minutes, stirring occasionally.

Add orzo and cook until tender, about 10 minutes. Season with salt and pepper.

Serve hot, garnished with fresh basil or parsley and optional grated Parmesan cheese.

Nutritional Information: 210 calories, 7g protein, 38g carbohydrates, 4g fat, 4g fiber, 0mg cholesterol, 570mg sodium, 400mg potassium.

Turkish Ezogelin Soup

INGREDIENTS

- 1/2 cup red lentils
- 1/4 cup fine bulgur
- 4 cups chicken broth
- 1 tablespoon tomato paste
- 1 small onion, finely chopped
- 2 cloves garlic, minced
- 1 tablespoon olive oil
- 1 teaspoon paprika
- 1 teaspoon dried mint
- 1/2 teaspoon ground cumin
- Salt and pepper to taste
- Lemon wedges, for serving
- Fresh parsley, chopped

Prep Time: 10 min

Cook Time: 25 min

Serves: 4

DIRECTIONS

Rinse the lentils and bulgur under cold water until the water runs clear. Drain well.

In a large pot, heat olive oil over medium heat. Add chopped onion and garlic, and sauté until softened, about 3-4 minutes.

Stir in tomato paste, paprika, mint, and cumin. Cook for another 2 minutes.

Add the rinsed lentils, bulgur, and broth to the pot. Bring to a boil, then reduce heat and simmer for 20 minutes or until the lentils are tender.

Season with salt and pepper to taste. If the soup is too thick, add more broth or water to reach your desired consistency.

Serve hot with a squeeze of lemon juice and garnished with fresh parsley.

Nutritional Information: 180 calories, 7g protein, 29g carbohydrates, 5g fat, 6g fiber, 0mg cholesterol, 800mg sodium, 300mg potassium.

Greek Fasolada (White Bean Soup)

INGREDIENTS

- 1 cup dried white beans, soaked overnight
- 4 cups water or vegetable broth
- 2 tablespoons olive oil
- 1 onion, chopped
- 2 carrots, diced
- 2 celery stalks, diced
- 3 garlic cloves, minced
- 1 can (14.5 oz) diced tomatoes
- 1 bay leaf
- 1 teaspoon dried oregano
- Salt and pepper to taste
- Chopped fresh parsley, for garnish
- Lemon wedges, for serving

Prep Time: 10 min

Cook Time: 75 min

Serves: 4

DIRECTIONS

Drain and rinse the soaked white beans. In a large pot, combine the beans and water or vegetable broth. Bring to a boil over high heat, then reduce the heat to low, cover, and simmer for 45 minutes to 1 hour, or until the beans are tender.

In a separate skillet, heat olive oil over medium heat. Add chopped onion, carrots, and celery. Cook until the vegetables are softened, about 8-10 minutes.

Add garlic to the skillet and cook for an additional 1-2 minutes, until fragrant.

Transfer the cooked vegetables to the pot with the beans. Add diced tomatoes, bay leaf, and dried oregano. Season with salt and pepper to taste.

Continue to simmer the soup, uncovered, for an additional 15-20 minutes to allow the flavors to meld together. If the soup is too thick, you can add more water or broth to reach your desired consistency.

Serve hot, garnished with chopped fresh parsley and lemon wedges on the side.

Nutritional Information: 260 calories, 10g protein, 40g carbohydrates, 7g fat, 10g fiber, 0mg cholesterol, 480mg sodium, 800mg potassium.

Turkish Tarhana Soup

INGREDIENTS

- 1 cup tarhana mix
- 4 cups chicken or vegetable broth
- 1 tablespoon olive oil
- 1 onion, finely chopped
- 2 cloves garlic, minced
- 1 medium tomato, diced
- 1 tablespoon tomato paste
- 1 teaspoon paprika
- Salt and pepper to taste
- Chopped fresh parsley, for garnish
- Lemon wedges, for serving

Prep Time: 15 min

Cook Time: 25 min

Serves: 4

DIRECTIONS

In a bowl, mix the tarhana with 2 cups of broth until smooth. Set aside.

In a large pot, heat olive oil over medium heat. Add chopped onion and cook until translucent, about 5 minutes. Add garlic and cook for an additional 1-2 minutes.

Stir in diced tomato, tomato paste, and paprika. Cook for 3-4 minutes, until the tomatoes start to soften. Pour in the tarhana mixture and the remaining 2 cups of broth. Bring to a simmer and cook for 15-20 minutes, stirring occasionally, until the soup thickens and the flavors meld together.

Season with salt and pepper to taste. Serve hot, garnished with chopped fresh parsley and lemon wedges on the side.

Nutritional Information: 180 calories, 5g protein, 30g carbohydrates, 5g fat, 4g fiber, 0mg cholesterol, 800mg sodium, 300mg potassium.

Moroccan Chickpea Soup (Hummus Soup)

INGREDIENTS

- 2 tablespoons olive oil
- 1 onion, finely chopped
- 3 cloves garlic, minced
- 1 teaspoon ground cumin
- 1/2 teaspoon ground coriander
- 1/2 teaspoon smoked paprika
- 1 can chickpeas, drained and rinsed
- 4 cups vegetable broth
- 1/4 cup tahini
- 1/4 cup lemon juice
- Salt and pepper to taste
- Chopped fresh parsley, for garnish
- Lemon wedges, for serving

Prep Time: 10 min

Cook Time: 25 min

Serves: 4

DIRECTIONS

In a large pot, heat olive oil over medium heat. Add chopped onion and cook until softened, about 5 minutes.

Add minced garlic, ground cumin, ground coriander, smoked paprika. Cook for 1-2 minutes until fragrant.

Stir in the drained chickpeas and vegetable broth. Bring to a simmer and cook for 15 minutes.

In a small bowl, whisk together tahini and lemon juice until smooth. Gradually stir the tahini mixture into the soup until well combined.

Season with salt and pepper to taste. If the soup is too thick, you can add more broth or water to reach your desired consistency.

Serve hot, garnished with chopped fresh parsley and lemon wedges on the side.

Nutritional Information: 280 calories, 9g protein, 22g carbohydrates, 18g fat, 6g fiber, 0mg cholesterol, 800mg sodium, 320mg potassium.

Greek Fisherman's Soup (Kakavia)

INGREDIENTS

- 1 lb mixed fish fillets (such as cod, snapper, or halibut)
- 1/2 lb shrimp
- 1/4 cup olive oil
- 1 onion, finely chopped
- 2 cloves garlic, minced
- 1 carrot, diced
- 1 celery stalk, diced
- 1 potato, diced
- 1 can diced tomatoes
- 4 cups fish or seafood broth
- 1/4 cup dry white wine
- 1 bay leaf
- 1 teaspoon dried oregano
- Salt and pepper to taste
- Chopped fresh parsley
- Lemon wedges

Prep Time: 15 min

Cook Time: 30 min

Serves: 4

DIRECTIONS

Cut fish fillets into chunks and peel and devein the shrimps.

In a large pot, heat olive oil over medium heat. Add chopped onion and cook until softened, about 5 minutes. Add garlic and cook for an additional 1-2 minutes.

Add diced carrot, celery, and potato. Cook for 5 minutes, stirring occasionally.

Stir in diced tomatoes, fish or seafood broth, wine, bay leaf, and dried oregano. Bring to a simmer and cook for 15 minutes, or until the vegetables are tender.

Add the mixed fish fillets and shrimp to the pot. Cook for 5-7 minutes, or until the fish is cooked through and the shrimp are pink and opaque.

Season with salt and pepper to taste. Remove the bay leaf.

Serve hot, garnished with chopped fresh parsley and lemon wedges on the side.

Nutritional Information: 320 calories, 30g protein, 15g carbohydrates, 15g fat, 2g fiber, 90mg cholesterol, 800mg sodium, 600mg potassium.

Italian Stracciatella Soup

INGREDIENTS

- 4 cups chicken or vegetable broth
- 2 large eggs
- 2 tablespoons grated Parmesan cheese
- 2 tablespoons chopped fresh parsley
- Salt and pepper to taste
- Freshly grated nutmeg (optional)
- 1/4 cup uncooked small pasta (such as orzo or ditalini)

Prep Time: 10 min

Cook Time: 15 min

Serves: 4

DIRECTIONS

In a medium saucepan, bring the chicken or vegetable broth to a gentle boil over medium heat.

In a mixing bowl, whisk together the eggs, grated Parmesan cheese, chopped fresh parsley, salt, and pepper until well combined.

Gradually pour the egg mixture into the simmering broth while stirring continuously with a fork or whisk to create thin ribbons of cooked egg.

Add freshly grated nutmeg, if using, and stir in the uncooked small pasta. Cook for an additional 8-10 minutes, or until the pasta is tender.

Taste and adjust the seasoning with salt and pepper if needed.

Serve hot, garnished with grated Parmesan cheese and fresh parsley if desired.

Nutritional Information: 120 calories, 7g protein, 13g carbohydrates, 5g fat, 1g fiber, 105mg cholesterol, 800mg sodium, 60mg potassium.

Turkish Red Pepper and Lentil Soup (Biber Çorbası)

INGREDIENTS

- 1 cup red lentils, rinsed and drained
- 2 tablespoons olive oil
- 1 onion, finely chopped
- 2 cloves garlic, minced
- 2 red bell peppers, diced
- 1 teaspoon paprika
- 1/2 teaspoon ground cumin
- 1/4 teaspoon red pepper flakes (optional)
- 4 cups vegetable or chicken broth
- Salt and pepper to taste
- Fresh parsley, chopped, for garnish
- Lemon wedges, for serving

Prep Time: 10 min   Cook Time: 25 min   Serves: 4

DIRECTIONS

Heat the olive oil in a large pot over medium heat. Add the chopped onion and minced garlic, and cook until softened, about 3-4 minutes. Stir in the diced red bell peppers and cook for another 3-4 minutes until they begin to soften.

Add the rinsed red lentils, paprika, ground cumin, and red pepper flakes (if using). Stir to combine with the vegetables and spices. Pour in the vegetable or chicken broth and bring the mixture to a boil. Reduce the heat to low, cover, and simmer for about 15-20 minutes, or until the lentils are tender.

Use an immersion blender to blend the soup until smooth, or transfer the soup in batches to a blender and blend until smooth.

Season with salt and pepper to taste. Serve hot, garnished with chopped fresh parsley and lemon wedges on the side.

Nutritional Information: 220 calories, 10g protein, 33g carbohydrates, 6g fat, 10g fiber, 0mg cholesterol, 600mg sodium, 650mg potassium.

Moroccan Tomato Soup with Chickpeas and Rice

INGREDIENTS

- 1 tablespoon olive oil
- 1 onion, chopped
- 2 cloves garlic, minced
- 1 can diced tomatoes
- 4 cups vegetable broth
- 1/2 cup uncooked white rice
- 1 can (15 oz) chickpeas, drained and rinsed
- 1 teaspoon ground cumin
- 1/2 teaspoon ground cinnamon
- 1/2 teaspoon paprika
- Salt and pepper to taste
- Fresh cilantro, chopped, for garnish

Prep Time: 10 min   Cook Time: 25 min   Serves: 4

DIRECTIONS

Heat olive oil in a large pot over medium heat. Add chopped onion and minced garlic, and sauté until softened, about 3-4 minutes.

Stir in diced tomatoes (with their juices), vegetable broth, uncooked rice, chickpeas, ground cumin, ground cinnamon, and paprika.

Bring the mixture to a boil, then reduce the heat to low, cover, and simmer for about 20-25 minutes, or until the rice is cooked and the soup has thickened slightly.

Season with salt and pepper to taste.

Serve hot, garnished with chopped fresh cilantro.

Nutritional Information: 250 calories, 8g protein, 44g carbohydrates, 4g fat, 6g fiber, 0mg cholesterol, 800mg sodium, 400mg potassium.

Italian Creamy Tomato Basil Soup

INGREDIENTS

- 2 tablespoons olive oil
- 1 onion, chopped
- 2 cloves garlic, minced
- 2 cans diced tomatoes
- 1 cup vegetable broth
- 1/2 cup heavy cream
- 1/4 cup fresh basil leaves, chopped
- 1 teaspoon dried oregano
- Salt and pepper to taste
- Grated Parmesan cheese, for serving
- Fresh basil leaves, for garnish

 Prep Time: 10 min

 Cook Time: 25 min

 Serves: 4

DIRECTIONS

Heat olive oil in a large pot over medium heat. Add chopped onion and minced garlic, and sauté until softened, about 3-4 minutes.

Stir in diced tomatoes, vegetable broth, dried oregano, and salt and pepper to taste. Bring to a boil, then reduce heat and simmer for about 15 minutes.

Use an immersion blender to puree the soup until smooth. Alternatively, transfer the soup in batches to a blender and blend until smooth, then return to the pot.

Stir in heavy cream and chopped fresh basil. Simmer for 5-10 minutes.

Serve hot, garnished with grated Parmesan cheese and fresh basil leaves.

Nutritional Information: 280 calories, 5g protein, 20g carbohydrates, 22g fat, 4g fiber, 50mg cholesterol, 650mg sodium, 500mg potassium.

Turkish Chicken & Vegetable Soup

INGREDIENTS

- 1 tablespoon olive oil
- 1 onion, finely chopped
- 2 carrots, diced
- 2 celery stalks, diced
- 2 garlic cloves, minced
- 1 teaspoon paprika
- 1/2 teaspoon ground cumin
- 1/2 teaspoon dried thyme
- 4 cups chicken broth
- 2 cups cooked chicken breast, shredded
- 1 cup diced tomatoes
- Salt and pepper to taste
- Fresh parsley, chopped, for garnish
- Lemon wedges, for serving

 Prep Time: 15 min

 Cook Time: 25 min

 Serves: 4

DIRECTIONS

In a large pot, heat olive oil over medium heat. Add chopped onion, diced carrots, and diced celery. Sauté until vegetables are softened, about 5-6 minutes.

Add minced garlic, paprika, ground cumin, and dried thyme. Cook for another 2 minutes until fragrant.

Pour in chicken broth and bring to a simmer. Add shredded chicken breast and diced tomatoes. Simmer for 15 minutes.

Season with salt and pepper to taste. Adjust seasoning if necessary.

Ladle the soup into serving bowls. Garnish with chopped fresh parsley and serve with lemon wedges on the side.

Nutritional Information: 200 calories, 20g protein, 15g carbohydrates, 6g fat, 3g fiber, 30mg cholesterol, 800mg sodium, 550mg potassium.

Italian Sicilian Fish Soup (Zuppa di Pesce)

INGREDIENTS

- 1 tablespoon olive oil
- 1 onion, finely chopped
- 2 garlic cloves, minced
- 1 red bell pepper, diced
- 1 fennel bulb, thinly sliced
- 1/2 teaspoon red pepper flakes
- 1 teaspoon dried oregano
- 1 teaspoon dried basil
- 1/2 cup dry white wine
- 1 can diced tomatoes
- 3 cups fish or seafood stock
- 1 pound mixed seafood (such as shrimp, mussels, clams, and fish fillets)
- Salt and pepper to taste
- Fresh parsley, chopped
- Crusty bread, for serving

 Prep Time: 15 min

 Cook Time: 25 min

Serves: 4

DIRECTIONS

Clean and devein the seafood.

In a large pot, heat olive oil over medium heat. Add chopped onion and minced garlic, sauté until softened, about 3-4 minutes.

Add diced red bell pepper, thinly sliced fennel, red pepper flakes, dried oregano, and dried basil. Cook for another 5 minutes until vegetables are tender.

Pour in dry white wine and cook until it reduces slightly, about 2 minutes.

Add diced tomatoes and fish or seafood. Bring to a simmer and cook for 10 minutes to allow flavors to meld. Add mixed seafood to the pot and cook for about 5-7 minutes. Season with salt and pepper to taste.

Ladle the soup into serving bowls, garnish with chopped fresh parsley, and serve with crusty bread on the side.

Nutritional Information: 250 calories, 25g protein, 20g carbohydrates, 8g fat, 3g fiber, 60mg cholesterol, 800mg sodium, 600mg potassium.

Turkish Lamb Soup (Kuzu Etli Sebzeli Çorba)

INGREDIENTS

- 1 tablespoon olive oil
- 1 onion, finely chopped
- 2 garlic cloves, minced
- 1 pound lamb stew meat, diced
- 2 carrots, diced
- 2 potatoes, diced
- 1 zucchini, diced
- 4 cups beef or vegetable broth
- 1 teaspoon paprika
- 1 teaspoon ground cumin
- Salt and pepper to taste
- Fresh parsley, chopped, for garnish

 Prep Time: 15 min

 Cook Time: 40 min

Serves: 4

DIRECTIONS

Heat olive oil in a large pot over medium heat. Add chopped onion and minced garlic, sauté until softened, about 3-4 minutes.

Add diced lamb stew meat to the pot and cook until browned on all sides, about 5-7 minutes. Stir in diced carrots, potatoes, and zucchini. Cook for 5 minutes.

Pour in beef or vegetable broth and bring to a simmer. Add paprika, ground cumin, salt, and pepper. Cover and simmer for 25-30 minutes until vegetables are tender and lamb is cooked through.

Taste and adjust seasoning. Serve hot, garnished with chopped fresh parsley.

Nutritional Information: 350 calories, 25g protein, 30g carbohydrates, 15g fat, 5g fiber, 60mg cholesterol, 800mg sodium, 900mg potassium.

Moroccan Carrot and Coriander Soup

INGREDIENTS

- 1 tablespoon olive oil
- 1 onion, chopped
- 2 garlic cloves, minced
- 1 pound carrots, peeled and chopped
- 4 cups vegetable broth
- 1 teaspoon ground coriander
- 1 teaspoon ground cumin
- 1/2 teaspoon ground turmeric
- Salt and pepper to taste
- Chopped coriander leaves
- Yogurt (optional)

 Prep Time: 10 min

 Cook Time: 25 min

 Serves: 4

DIRECTIONS

Heat olive oil in a large pot over medium heat. Add chopped onion and garlic, sauté until softened, about 3-4 minutes. Add chopped carrots to the pot and cook for another 5 minutes, stirring occasionally. Pour in vegetable broth and bring to a simmer. Add ground coriander, cumin, turmeric, salt, and pepper. Cover and simmer for 15-20 minutes until the carrots are tender.
Using a blender puree the soup until smooth.
Taste and adjust seasoning if needed. Serve hot, garnished with chopped fresh coriander leaves and a dollop of yogurt if desired.

Nutritional Information: 120 calories, 2g protein, 15g carbohydrates, 6g fat, 4g fiber, 0mg cholesterol, 800mg sodium, 600mg potassium.

Beans

Italian Pasta with Cannellini Beans and Garlic

INGREDIENTS

- 8 oz pasta (such as penne or rigatoni)
- 1 can (15 oz) cannellini beans, drained and rinsed
- 4 cloves garlic, minced
- 1/4 cup extra virgin olive oil
- 1/2 teaspoon red pepper flakes (optional)
- Salt and black pepper to taste
- Grated Parmesan cheese, for serving
- Chopped fresh parsley, for garnish

 Prep Time: 10 min

 Cook Time: 20 min

 Serves: 4

DIRECTIONS

Cook the pasta until al dente. Drain and set aside, reserving 1/2 cup of pasta water. In a large skillet, heat the olive oil over medium heat. Add the garlic and red pepper flakes (if using). Cook for 1-2 minutes until the garlic is just starting to turn golden. Add the drained cannellini beans to the skillet. Cook for 3-4 minutes, stirring occasionally, until the beans are starting to soften. Add the cooked pasta to the same skillet. Toss everything together, adding a splash of pasta water if needed to loosen the sauce. Season the pasta with salt and black pepper to taste. Serve hot, garnished with grated Parmesan cheese and chopped fresh parsley.

Nutritional Information: 420 calories, 14g protein, 63g carbohydrates, 12g fat, 8g fiber, 0mg cholesterol, 450mg sodium, 300mg potassium.

Greek Gigantes Plaki (Giant Beans in Tomato Sauce)

INGREDIENTS

- 1 cup dried giant beans, soaked overnight and drained
- 1 onion, finely chopped
- 3 garlic cloves, minced
- 1 can (14 ounces) diced tomatoes
- 2 tablespoons tomato paste
- 1/4 cup extra virgin olive oil
- 1 teaspoon dried oregano
- 1 teaspoon dried thyme
- 1 teaspoon paprika
- Salt and pepper to taste
- Fresh parsley, chopped, for garnish

 Prep Time: 15 min

 Cook Time: 60 min

 Serves: 4

DIRECTIONS

Preheat the oven to 350°F (175°C).

In a pot, cover the beans with water and bring to a boil. Reduce heat and simmer for 30-40 minutes, until the beans are tender but still firm. Drain and set aside.

In a separate skillet, heat olive oil over medium heat. Add chopped onion and minced garlic, sauté until softened and fragrant, about 5 minutes.

Stir in diced tomatoes, tomato paste, dried oregano, dried thyme, paprika, salt, and pepper. Cook for another 5 minutes, allowing the flavors to meld.

Add the cooked giant beans to the tomato mixture, stirring gently to combine. Transfer the mixture to a baking dish. Cover the baking dish with aluminum foil and bake in the preheated oven for 30 minutes. Remove the foil and bake for an additional 15-20 minutes, until the sauce is thickened and bubbly.

Serve hot, garnished with chopped fresh parsley.

Nutritional Information: 300 calories, 8g protein, 42g carbohydrates, 12g fat, 10g fiber, 0mg cholesterol, 400mg sodium, 800mg potassium.

Mediterranean White Bean and Tuna Salad

INGREDIENTS

- 2 cans (15 oz each) white beans, drained and rinsed
- 2 cans (5 oz each) tuna in water, drained
- 1/2 red onion, finely chopped
- 1 cup cherry tomatoes, halved
- 1/4 cup chopped fresh parsley
- 2 tablespoons lemon juice
- 2 tablespoons extra virgin olive oil
- Salt and black pepper to taste
- Optional: olives, capers, feta cheese, for garnish

 Prep Time: 10 min

 Cook Time: 0 min

 Serves: 4

DIRECTIONS

In a large mixing bowl, combine the drained and rinsed white beans, drained tuna, chopped red onion, halved cherry tomatoes, and chopped fresh parsley.

Drizzle the lemon juice and extra virgin olive oil over the salad ingredients.

Season the salad with salt and black pepper to taste. Toss everything together until well combined.

Taste and adjust the seasoning, if needed. If desired, garnish the salad with olives, capers, or crumbled feta cheese.

Serve the Mediterranean White Bean and Tuna Salad immediately, or refrigerate for 30 minutes to allow the flavors to meld before serving.

Nutritional Information: 330 calories, 30g protein, 32g carbohydrates, 10g fat, 9g fiber, 30mg cholesterol, 450mg sodium, 600mg potassium.

Italian Pasta e Fagioli

INGREDIENTS

- 1 tablespoon olive oil
- 4 slices bacon, chopped
- 1 onion, diced
- 2 cloves garlic, minced
- 1 carrot, diced
- 1 celery stalk, diced
- 1 can diced tomatoes
- 4 cups chicken broth
- 1 can cannellini beans
- 1 teaspoon dried oregano
- 1 teaspoon dried basil
- 1/2 teaspoon dried thyme
- Salt and pepper to taste
- 1 cup small pasta (ditalini)
- Grated Parmesan cheese
- Fresh parsley, chopped

 Prep Time: 10 min

 Cook Time: 25 min

Serves: 4

DIRECTIONS

In a large pot, heat olive oil over medium heat. Add chopped bacon and cook until crispy, about 5 minutes. Add diced onion, minced garlic, diced carrot, and diced celery to the pot. Sauté until vegetables are softened, about 5-7 minutes.

Stir in diced tomatoes (with juices), chicken or vegetable broth, cannellini beans, dried oregano, dried basil, dried thyme, salt, and pepper. Bring to a boil.

Reduce heat and simmer for 10 minutes to allow the flavors to meld together.

Add the small pasta to the pot and cook until al dente, according to package instructions, stirring occasionally.

Once the pasta is cooked, taste and adjust the seasoning with salt and pepper.

Serve hot, garnished with grated Parmesan cheese and chopped fresh parsley.

Nutritional Information: 380 calories, 18g protein, 49g carbohydrates, 12g fat, 8g fiber, 10mg cholesterol, 900mg sodium, 400mg potassium.

Spanish Lentil Stew with Chorizo

INGREDIENTS

- 1 cup dry green or brown lentils
- 4 cups water or vegetable broth
- 1 tablespoon olive oil
- 1 onion, chopped
- 2 cloves garlic, minced
- 2 carrots, diced
- 2 stalks celery, diced
- 8 ounces chorizo sausage, sliced
- 1 bay leaf
- 1 teaspoon smoked paprika
- Salt and pepper to taste
- Fresh parsley, chopped, for garnish (optional)

 Prep Time: 10 min

 Cook Time: 40 min

Serves: 4

DIRECTIONS

Rinse the lentils under cold water and drain.

In a large pot, heat the olive oil over medium heat. Add the chopped onion, garlic, carrots, and celery. Sauté until the vegetables are softened, about 5 minutes.

Add the sliced chorizo sausage to the pot and cook until browned, about 5 minutes. Stir in the rinsed lentils, water or vegetable broth, bay leaf, and smoked paprika. Bring the mixture to a boil.

Reduce the heat to low, cover, and simmer for about 30 minutes, or until the lentils are tender.

Season with salt and pepper to taste. Remove the bay leaf before serving.

Garnish with chopped fresh parsley if desired, and serve hot.

Nutritional Information: 350 calories, 18g protein, 35g carbohydrates, 16g fat, 12g fiber, 25mg cholesterol, 700mg sodium, 600mg potassium.

Greek Fasolakia (Green Bean Stew)

INGREDIENTS

- 1 lb fresh green beans, trimmed and cut
- 2 tablespoons olive oil
- 1 onion, finely chopped
- 2 cloves garlic, minced
- 2 medium tomatoes, chopped
- 1 teaspoon dried oregano
- 1 teaspoon dried thyme
- Salt and pepper to taste
- 1 cup vegetable or chicken broth
- Juice of 1 lemon
- Crumbled feta cheese for serving (optional)

 Prep Time: 15 min

 Cook Time: 30 min

 Serves: 4

DIRECTIONS

In a large skillet or pot, heat the olive oil over medium heat. Add the chopped onion and garlic, and sauté until softened and fragrant, about 3-4 minutes.

Add the tomatoes to the skillet and cook for another 4-5 minutes, until they start to break down and release their juices. Stir in the beans, oregano, and thyme. Season with salt and pepper to taste. Cook for 5 minutes, stirring occasionally.

Pour in the vegetable or chicken broth and bring the mixture to a simmer. Reduce the heat to low, cover, and let it simmer for 20 minutes until the beans are tender.

Once the green beans are cooked, stir in the lemon juice and adjust the seasoning if needed. Serve the Fasolakia hot, garnished with crumbled feta cheese if desired.

Nutritional Information: 120 calories, 3g protein, 15g carbohydrates, 6g fat, 5g fiber, 0mg cholesterol, 350mg sodium, 400mg potassium.

Spanish Fabada Asturiana (White Bean Stew)

INGREDIENTS

- 1 cup dried white beans (such as Great Northern or cannellini), soaked overnight
- 4 cups chicken broth
- 4 oz chorizo sausage, sliced
- 4 oz bacon, chopped
- 1 onion, chopped
- 2 cloves garlic, minced
- 1 bay leaf
- 1 teaspoon paprika
- 1/2 teaspoon ground cumin
- Salt and pepper to taste
- Chopped fresh parsley, for garnish

 Prep Time: 15 min

 Cook Time: 90 min

 Serves: 4

DIRECTIONS

Drain the beans and rinse them under cold water. In a large pot, combine the beans and chicken broth. Bring to a boil, then reduce heat and simmer for 1 hour.

In a separate skillet, cook the chorizo sausage and bacon over medium heat until they start to brown and release their fat, about 5-7 minutes. Add the onion and garlic. Cook until the onion is translucent, about 3-4 minutes.

Transfer the cooked chorizo, bacon, onion, and garlic mixture to the pot with the cooked white beans. Add the bay leaf, paprika, ground cumin, salt, and pepper. Stir to combine.

Simmer the stew for additional 30 minutes to allow the flavors to meld together and the stew to thicken slightly.

Remove the bay leaf before serving. Garnish each bowl with chopped fresh parsley.

Nutritional Information: 420 calories, 20g protein, 40g carbohydrates, 20g fat, 10g fiber, 25mg cholesterol, 800mg sodium, 900mg potassium.

Italian Pasta e Ceci (Pasta with Chickpeas)

INGREDIENTS

- 8 oz dried small pasta (ditalini or small shells)
- 1 can (15 oz) chickpeas, drained and rinsed
- 2 tablespoons olive oil
- 1 small onion, chopped
- 2 cloves garlic, minced
- 1 can diced tomatoes
- 3 cups vegetable or chicken broth
- 1 teaspoon dried oregano
- 1 teaspoon dried basil
- Salt and pepper to taste
- Grated Parmesan cheese for serving (optional)
- Chopped fresh parsley for garnish (optional)

Prep Time: 10 min

Cook Time: 20 min

Serves: 4

DIRECTIONS

Cook the pasta according to package instructions in a large pot of salted boiling water until al dente. Drain and set aside.

In the same pot, heat the olive oil over medium heat. Add the chopped onion and garlic, and sauté until softened and fragrant, about 3-4 minutes.

Add the diced tomatoes (with their juices), chickpeas, oregano, and basil to the pot. Season with salt and pepper to taste. Cook for 5 minutes, stirring occasionally.

Pour in the broth and bring the mixture to a simmer. Let it simmer for about 10 minutes to allow the flavors to meld together and the chickpeas to soften slightly.

Add the cooked pasta to the pot and stir to combine. Cook for an additional 2-3 minutes, or until the pasta is heated through.

Serve hot, garnished with grated Parmesan cheese and chopped parsley if desired.

Nutritional Information: 350 calories, 12g protein, 55g carbohydrates, 9g fat, 8g fiber, 0mg cholesterol, 600mg sodium, 300mg potassium.

Spanish Judías Verdes con Tomate

INGREDIENTS

- 1 lb fresh green beans, trimmed and washed
- 2 tablespoons olive oil
- 2 cloves garlic, minced
- 1 small onion, finely chopped
- 2 large tomatoes, diced
- 1 teaspoon paprika
- Salt and pepper to taste
- Chopped fresh parsley, for garnish (optional)

Prep Time: 10 min

Cook Time: 15 min

Serves: 4

DIRECTIONS

In a large skillet, heat the olive oil over medium heat. Add the minced garlic and chopped onion, and sauté until softened and fragrant, about 2-3 minutes.

Add the diced tomatoes to the skillet and cook for another 3-4 minutes, until they begin to break down and release their juices.

Stir in the green beans and paprika. Season with salt and pepper to taste. Cover the skillet and cook for about 8-10 minutes, or until the green beans are tender but still crisp.

Once the green beans are cooked to your desired tenderness, remove the skillet from the heat. Taste and adjust the seasoning if needed.

Transfer the Spanish Green Beans with Tomato to a serving dish, garnish with chopped fresh parsley if desired, and serve hot as a delicious side dish.

Nutritional Information: 90 calories, 2g protein, 9g carbohydrates, 6g fat, 3g fiber, 0mg cholesterol, 150mg sodium, 380mg potassium.

Spanish Habas con Jamón (Broad Beans with Ham)

INGREDIENTS

- 1 lb fresh broad beans (fava beans), shelled
- 4 oz serrano ham or prosciutto, diced
- 2 tablespoons olive oil
- 1 small onion, finely chopped
- 2 cloves garlic, minced
- 1/2 teaspoon smoked paprika
- Salt and pepper to taste
- Chopped fresh parsley for garnish (optional)
- Lemon wedges for serving (optional)

Prep Time: 10 min

Cook Time: 20 min

Serves: 4

DIRECTIONS

Blanch the beans in boiling water for 1-2 minutes, then transfer to a bowl of ice water to stop cooking. Peel off the outer skins and set aside.

In a large skillet, heat the olive oil over medium heat. Add the diced serrano ham or prosciutto and cook until lightly browned and crispy, about 3-4 minutes. Add the chopped onion to the skillet and cook until softened and translucent, about 3 minutes. Stir in the garlic and cook for 1 minute, until fragrant.

Add the broad beans and the smoked paprika. Season with salt and pepper. Cook, stirring occasionally, for 8-10 minutes, until the beans are tender but still crisp.

Once the beans are cooked, remove the skillet from the heat. Garnish with chopped fresh parsley if desired, and serve hot with lemon wedges on the side.

Nutritional Information: 180 calories, 10g protein, 15g carbohydrates, 8g fat, 6g fiber, 15mg cholesterol, 480mg sodium, 400mg potassium.

Greek Fava Santorinis (Yellow Split Pea Puree)

INGREDIENTS

- 1 cup yellow split peas
- 4 cups water
- 1 onion, chopped
- 2 cloves garlic, minced
- 1 bay leaf
- 2 tablespoons olive oil
- Salt and pepper to taste
- Lemon wedges for serving
- Chopped fresh parsley for garnish

Prep Time: 10 min

Cook Time: 30 min

Serves: 4

DIRECTIONS

Rinse the yellow split peas under cold water. In a large pot, combine the split peas, water, chopped onion, minced garlic, and bay leaf. Bring the mixture to a boil over high heat. Once boiling, reduce the heat to low and let simmer, partially covered, for about 25-30 minutes or until the split peas are tender and mushy.

Remove the bay leaf from the pot. Use a blender to mix it until smooth and creamy. Return the pureed mixture to the pot if necessary. Stir in the olive oil and season with salt and pepper to taste.

Cook over low heat for an additional 5 minutes, stirring occasionally, until heated through and well combined.

Serve the fava hot, garnished with chopped fresh parsley and lemon wedges on the side.

Nutritional Information: 190 calories, 9g protein, 30g carbohydrates, 5g fat, 8g fiber, 0mg cholesterol, 480mg sodium, 350mg potassium.

Chickpeas with Spinach

INGREDIENTS

- 2 cans chickpeas, drained
- 8 oz fresh spinach leaves, washed and chopped
- 2 tablespoons olive oil
- 1 onion, finely chopped
- 3 cloves garlic, minced
- 1 teaspoon ground cumin
- 1/2 teaspoon paprika
- 1/4 teaspoon cayenne pepper (optional)
- Salt and pepper to taste
- 1 cup vegetable broth
- 1 tablespoon lemon juice
- Lemon wedges (optional)

 Prep Time: 10 min

 Cook Time: 20 min

Serves: 4

DIRECTIONS

In a large skillet, heat the olive oil over medium heat. Add the onion and cook until softened and translucent, about 3-4 minutes. Add the garlic cook for 1-2 minutes. Stir in the ground cumin, paprika, and cayenne pepper (if using). Cook for another 1-2 minutes to toast the spices. Add the drained chickpeas and stir to coat them in the spices. Pour in the vegetable broth and bring to a simmer.

Once simmering, add the chopped spinach and stir until wilted and heat through, about 3-4 minutes. Season with salt and pepper. Stir in the lemon juice for a hint of brightness. Serve hot with lemon wedges on the side.

Nutritional Information: 280 calories, 12g protein, 40g carbohydrates, 10g fat, 10g fiber, 0mg cholesterol, 600mg sodium, 700mg potassium.

Grains

Israeli Couscous with Herbs

INGREDIENTS

- 1 cup Israeli couscous (also known as pearl couscous)
- 2 cups vegetable broth
- 1 tablespoon olive oil
- 1/4 cup chopped fresh parsley
- 1/4 cup chopped fresh basil
- 1/4 cup chopped fresh mint
- 1 lemon, zested and juiced
- Salt and black pepper to taste

 Prep Time: 5 min

 Cook Time: 15 min

 Serves: 4

DIRECTIONS

In a medium saucepan, heat the olive oil over medium heat. Add the Israeli couscous and toast until lightly golden, about 5 minutes, stirring frequently.

Add the vegetable broth and bring to a boil. Reduce heat to low, cover, and simmer until the couscous is tender and the liquid is absorbed, about 10 minutes.

Remove from heat and stir in the chopped herbs, lemon zest, and lemon juice. Season with salt and pepper to taste.

Serve warm as a side dish or cool as a salad base.

Nutritional Information: 210 calories, 6g protein, 42g carbohydrates, 4g fat, 3g fiber, 0mg cholesterol, 480mg sodium, 220mg potassium.

Greek Lemon Rice

INGREDIENTS

- 1 cup long-grain white rice
- 2 cups chicken broth
- Zest of 1 lemon
- 3 tablespoons lemon juice
- 2 tablespoons olive oil
- 1 clove garlic, minced
- 1/2 teaspoon salt
- 1/4 teaspoon black pepper
- 1/4 cup fresh parsley, finely chopped
- 1 tablespoon fresh dill, chopped (optional)

 Prep Time: 5 min

 Cook Time: 20 min

 Serves: 4

DIRECTIONS

In a medium saucepan, heat the olive oil over medium heat. Add the minced garlic and sauté until fragrant, about 1 minute.

Stir in the rice and cook for 2 minutes until slightly toasted.

Add the chicken broth, lemon zest, lemon juice, salt, and pepper to the saucepan.

Bring to a boil, then reduce the heat to low, cover, and let simmer until the rice is tender and the liquid has been absorbed, about 20 minutes.

Remove from heat, fluff the rice with a fork, and stir in the fresh parsley and dill.

Nutritional Information: 210 calories, 4g protein, 37g carbohydrates, 5g fat, 1g fiber, 0mg cholesterol, 450mg sodium, 55mg potassium.

Spanakorizo (Greek Spinach and Rice)

INGREDIENTS

- 1 cup long-grain white rice
- 2 tablespoons olive oil
- 1 onion, finely chopped
- 2 cloves garlic, minced
- 1 pound fresh spinach, washed and chopped
- 1 cup vegetable broth or water
- 1 teaspoon dried dill
- Salt and pepper to taste
- Lemon wedges, for serving

Prep Time: 10 min

Cook Time: 25 min

Serves: 4

DIRECTIONS

Rinse the rice under cold water until the water runs clear. Drain and set aside.

In a large skillet, heat the olive oil over medium heat. Add the chopped onion and minced garlic. Sauté until softened, about 3 minutes.

Add the chopped spinach to the skillet and cook until wilted, about 5 minutes.

Stir in the rice, vegetable broth or water, and dried dill. Season with salt and pepper to taste.

Bring the mixture to a boil, then reduce the heat to low. Cover and simmer until the rice is tender and the liquid is absorbed, about 15 minutes.

Remove from heat and let it sit, covered, for 5 minutes. Fluff the rice with a fork.

Serve hot with lemon wedges on the side.

Nutritional Information: 220 calories, 5g protein, 35g carbohydrates, 7g fat, 3g fiber, 0mg cholesterol, 300mg sodium, 500mg potassium.

Classic Italian Risotto

INGREDIENTS

- 1 cup Arborio rice
- 4 cups chicken or vegetable broth, heated
- 1/2 cup dry white wine
- 1 small onion, finely chopped
- 2 tablespoons unsalted butter
- 2 tablespoons olive oil
- 1/3 cup grated Parmesan cheese
- Salt and black pepper to taste
- 2 cloves garlic, minced
- Optional: 1 cup mushrooms, sliced (for variation)

Prep Time: 5 min

Cook Time: 30 min

Serves: 4

DIRECTIONS

In a large skillet or saucepan, heat the olive oil and 1 tablespoon of butter over medium heat. Add the onion and garlic, sauté until translucent, about 5 minutes. Add the rice, stirring constantly, until the grains begin to turn golden, about 2 minutes.

Pour in the white wine, stirring continuously, until the wine has been absorbed by the rice. Then start adding the heated broth, one ladle at a time, allowing each ladle to be absorbed before adding the next. Stir frequently to prevent sticking.

After about 18-20 minutes, when the rice is tender but still slightly firm to the bite, remove from heat. Stir in the remaining butter and the Parmesan cheese. Season with salt and pepper to taste.

Serve hot, garnished with additional Parmesan or herbs if desired.

Nutritional Information: 350 calories, 9g protein, 47g carbohydrates, 12g fat, 1g fiber, 25mg cholesterol, 900mg sodium, 125mg potassium.

Couscous with Roasted Vegetables

INGREDIENTS

- 1 cup couscous
- 1 zucchini, cut into bite-sized pieces
- 1 bell pepper, any color, diced
- 1 red onion, chopped
- 1 carrot, peeled and diced
- 2 tablespoons olive oil
- 1/2 teaspoon salt
- 1/4 teaspoon black pepper
- 2 cups vegetable broth
- 1/4 cup fresh parsley, chopped
- Optional: feta cheese for garnish

Prep Time: 15 min

Cook Time: 25 min

Serves: 4

DIRECTIONS

Preheat the oven to 425°F (220°C). Toss zucchini, bell pepper, red onion, and carrot with olive oil, salt, and pepper. Spread the vegetables on a baking sheet and roast for about 20 minutes, until tender and lightly browned.

Meanwhile, bring the vegetable broth to a boil in a medium saucepan. Add the couscous, stir, then remove from heat. Cover and let stand for 5 minutes, or until all the liquid is absorbed.

Fluff the couscous with a fork and mix in the roasted vegetables and fresh parsley. Adjust seasoning with additional salt and pepper if needed.

Serve warm, garnished with crumbled feta cheese if using.

Nutritional Information: 290 calories, 8g protein, 52g carbohydrates, 7g fat, 5g fiber, 0mg cholesterol, 610mg sodium, 340mg potassium.

Bulgur Pilaf with Chickpeas

INGREDIENTS

- 1 cup bulgur wheat
- 1 can (15 ounces) chickpeas, drained and rinsed
- 1 large onion, finely chopped
- 2 cloves garlic, minced
- 2 tablespoons olive oil
- 2 cups vegetable broth
- 1/2 teaspoon ground cumin
- 1/2 teaspoon salt
- 1/4 teaspoon black pepper
- 1/4 cup fresh parsley, chopped
- Optional: 1/4 cup chopped nuts (e.g., almonds or pistachios) for garnish

 Prep Time: 10 min   Cook Time: 20 min   Serves: 4

DIRECTIONS

Heat the olive oil in a large skillet over medium heat. Add the onion and garlic, and sauté until the onion is translucent, about 5 minutes.

Stir in the bulgur and chickpeas, cook for another 2 minutes, then add the cumin, salt, and pepper.

Pour in the vegetable broth and bring to a boil. Reduce heat to low, cover, and simmer until the bulgur is tender and the liquid is absorbed, about 15 minutes.

Remove from heat and let sit covered for 5 minutes. Fluff with a fork, then stir in the chopped parsley.

Serve hot, garnished with nuts if using.

Nutritional Information: 330 calories, 11g protein, 53g carbohydrates, 9g fat, 13g fiber, 0mg cholesterol, 620mg sodium, 390mg potassium.

Mediterranean Rice Pilaf

INGREDIENTS

- 1 cup long-grain white rice
- 2 cups chicken or vegetable broth
- 1/2 cup diced red bell pepper
- 1/2 cup diced yellow bell pepper
- 1/2 cup diced zucchini
- 1/4 cup raisins
- 1/4 cup chopped almonds
- 2 tablespoons olive oil
- 1 teaspoon ground cumin
- 1/2 teaspoon salt
- 1/4 teaspoon black pepper
- 1/4 cup fresh parsley, chopped

Prep Time: 10 min   Cook Time: 20 min   Serves: 4

DIRECTIONS

Heat olive oil in a large skillet over medium heat. Add the red and yellow bell peppers, zucchini, and raisins. Sauté for about 5 minutes until the vegetables are slightly softened.

Stir in the rice, ground cumin, salt, and pepper, mixing well to coat the rice with the oil and spices.

Pour in the chicken or vegetable broth and bring to a boil. Reduce heat to low, cover, and simmer for 15-18 minutes, or until the rice is cooked and all the liquid is absorbed.

Remove from heat, fluff with a fork, and mix in the chopped parsley and almonds.

Nutritional Information: 310 calories, 7g protein, 51g carbohydrates, 9g fat, 3g fiber, 0mg cholesterol, 470mg sodium, 290mg potassium.

Baked Stuffed Tomatoes with Rice

INGREDIENTS

- 4 large tomatoes
- 1/2 cup cooked rice
- 1/4 cup finely chopped onion
- 2 cloves garlic, minced
- 1/4 cup chopped fresh parsley
- 1/4 cup grated Parmesan cheese
- 2 tablespoons olive oil
- 1/2 teaspoon salt
- 1/4 teaspoon black pepper
- Optional: 1/4 cup breadcrumbs for topping

Prep Time: 15 min

Cook Time: 30 min

Serves: 4

DIRECTIONS

Preheat the oven to 375°F (190°C). Cut the tops off the tomatoes and scoop out the pulp, leaving a shell. Chop the pulp and set aside.

In a skillet, heat 1 tablespoon of olive oil over medium heat. Add the onion and garlic, and sauté until soft, about 5 minutes. Mix in the tomato pulp, cooked rice, parsley, salt, and pepper. Cook for another 5 minutes.

Stuff each tomato shell with the rice mixture. Place the stuffed tomatoes in a baking dish. Sprinkle with Parmesan cheese and breadcrumbs if using. Drizzle with the remaining olive oil.

Bake in the preheated oven for about 20 minutes, or until the tomatoes are soft and the tops are golden brown.

Nutritional Information: 180 calories, 6g protein, 21g carbohydrates, 9g fat, 3g fiber, 5mg cholesterol, 370mg sodium, 340mg potassium.

Italian Polenta with Tomato Sauce

INGREDIENTS

- 1 cup polenta (cornmeal)
- 4 cups water
- 1 teaspoon salt
- 1 tablespoon olive oil
- 1/2 cup grated Parmesan cheese

  For the tomato sauce:
- 2 tablespoons olive oil
- 1 onion, finely chopped
- 2 cloves garlic, minced
- 1 can (14 ounces) crushed tomatoes
- 1 teaspoon dried basil
- 1/2 teaspoon sugar
- Salt and pepper to taste

Prep Time: 5 min

Cook Time: 30 min

Serves: 4

DIRECTIONS

In a large pot, bring water to a boil. Add salt and slowly whisk in the polenta. Reduce heat to low and cook, stirring often, until polenta is thick and creamy, about 20-25 minutes. Stir in 1 tablespoon olive oil and Parmesan cheese just before finishing.

For the sauce, heat olive oil in a saucepan over medium heat. Add onion and garlic, and sauté until onion is translucent, about 5 minutes. Add crushed tomatoes, basil, sugar, salt, and pepper. Simmer for 10 minutes, stirring occasionally.

Serve the creamy polenta topped with warm tomato sauce.

Nutritional Information: 330 calories, 8g protein, 49g carbohydrates, 12g fat, 5g fiber, 7mg cholesterol, 890mg sodium, 250mg potassium.

Farro Risotto with Mushrooms

INGREDIENTS

- 1 cup pearled farro
- 3 cups vegetable or chicken broth, heated
- 1 cup sliced mushrooms (such as cremini or shiitake)
- 1 small onion, finely chopped
- 2 cloves garlic, minced
- 2 tablespoons olive oil
- 1/2 cup dry white wine
- 1/4 cup grated Parmesan cheese
- 2 tablespoons fresh parsley, chopped
- Salt and black pepper to taste

 Prep Time: 10 min

 Cook Time: 30 min

 Serves: 4

DIRECTIONS

Heat the olive oil in a large skillet over medium heat. Add the onion and garlic, and sauté until the onion is translucent, about 5 minutes. Add the mushrooms and cook until they are browned and tender, about 5 more minutes.

Stir in the farro and cook for 1-2 minutes to toast lightly. Pour in the white wine and stir until mostly absorbed.

Gradually add the heated broth, one cup at a time, stirring frequently until each addition is absorbed before adding the next. Continue this process until the farro is creamy and cooked through, about 25-30 minutes.

Remove from heat, stir in the Parmesan cheese and parsley. Season with salt and pepper to taste. Serve warm.

Nutritional Information: 370 calories, 12g protein, 58g carbohydrates, 9g fat, 10g fiber, 7mg cholesterol, 640mg sodium, 300mg potassium.

Italian Tomato Risotto

INGREDIENTS

- 1 cup Arborio rice
- 1 can (14 ounces) diced tomatoes, with juice
- 3 cups chicken or vegetable broth, heated
- 1 small onion, finely chopped
- 2 cloves garlic, minced
- 2 tablespoons olive oil
- 1/2 cup dry white wine
- 1/4 cup grated Parmesan cheese
- 1/4 cup fresh basil, chopped
- Salt and black pepper to taste

 Prep Time: 10 min

 Cook Time: 25 min

 Serves: 4

DIRECTIONS

In a large skillet or saucepan, heat the olive oil over medium heat. Add the onion and garlic, and sauté until the onion is translucent, about 5 minutes.

Add the Arborio rice and stir until the grains are well coated and slightly translucent, about 2 minutes.

Pour in the white wine and stir until it is mostly absorbed by the rice. Add the diced tomatoes with their juice and a ladle of hot broth. Continue to cook, stirring frequently, adding more broth as it is absorbed.

After about 18 minutes, when the rice is creamy and al dente, remove from heat. Stir in the Parmesan cheese and chopped basil. Season with salt and pepper to taste.

Serve hot, garnished with additional basil or Parmesan if desired.

Nutritional Information: 320 calories, 9g protein, 51g carbohydrates, 7g fat, 2g fiber, 5mg cholesterol, 700mg sodium, 250mg potassium.

Couscous Stuffed Bell Peppers

INGREDIENTS

- 4 large bell peppers, tops cut off and seeds removed
- 1 cup couscous
- 1 1/4 cups boiling water
- 1 tablespoon olive oil
- 1/2 cup chopped onions
- 2 cloves garlic, minced
- 1 zucchini, diced
- 1/2 cup diced tomatoes
- 1/4 cup raisins
- 1/4 cup pine nuts
- 1 teaspoon cumin
- 1/2 teaspoon salt
- 1/4 teaspoon black pepper
- 1/4 cup parsley, chopped
- 1/4 cup feta cheese

Prep Time: 15 min

Cook Time: 30 min

Serves: 4

DIRECTIONS

Preheat oven to 375°F. Put the peppers in a baking dish keeping them upright.

In a bowl, pour boiling water over the couscous and cover with a plate. Let sit for 5 minutes, then fluff with a fork.

In a skillet, heat olive oil over medium heat. Add onions and garlic and sauté until soft, about 5 minutes. Add zucchini, tomatoes, raisins, nuts, cumin, salt, and pepper. Cook for another 5 minutes. Combine the vegetable mixture with the couscous, then stir in parsley and feta cheese if using.

Stuff the peppers with the couscous mixture, packing them tightly. Replace the tops of the peppers. Bake in the preheated oven for 25-30 minutes, until the peppers are tender and the filling is heated through.

Nutritional Information: 290 calories, 8g protein, 45g carbohydrates, 9g fat, 6g fiber, 5mg cholesterol, 330mg sodium, 500mg potassium.

Pastas

Spaghetti al Pomodoro (Tomato Basil Pasta)

INGREDIENTS

- 12 oz spaghetti
- 2 tablespoons extra virgin olive oil
- 3 cloves garlic, minced
- 1 can (28 oz) crushed tomatoes
- 1 teaspoon sugar
- Salt and pepper to taste
- 1/2 cup fresh basil leaves, chopped
- Grated Parmesan cheese for serving

Prep Time: 10 min

Cook Time: 20 min

Serves: 4

DIRECTIONS

Cook spaghetti until al dente. Drain and set aside.

In a large skillet, heat olive oil and add garlic and sauté for 1-2 minutes. Add tomatoes and sugar, salt and pepper. Simmer the sauce for 10-15 minutes until it thickens slightly. Stir in chopped basil and cook for an additional 2 minutes.

Toss the cooked spaghetti with the tomato sauce. Serve hot, garnished with grated Parmesan cheese.

Nutritional Information: 350 calories, 12g protein, 65g carbohydrates, 7g fat, 4g fiber, 0mg cholesterol, 320mg sodium, 410mg potassium.

Whole Wheat Spaghetti with Lemon, Basil & Salmon

INGREDIENTS

- 12 oz whole wheat spaghetti
- 2 tablespoons olive oil
- 2 cloves garlic, minced
- 1 lb salmon fillet, skin removed and cut into chunks
- Zest and juice of 1 large lemon
- 1/2 cup fresh basil leaves, chopped
- Salt and pepper to taste
- Grated Parmesan cheese for garnish (optional)

Prep Time: 10 min　　Cook Time: 20 min　　Serves: 4

DIRECTIONS

Cook the whole wheat spaghetti according to package instructions until al dente. Drain and set aside.

While the pasta cooks, heat olive oil in a large skillet over medium heat. Add the garlic and sauté until fragrant, about 1 minute.

Add the salmon chunks to the skillet and cook until they are opaque and slightly golden, about 5-7 minutes. Remove from heat.

Toss the cooked spaghetti with the salmon, adding the lemon zest, lemon juice, and fresh basil. Season with salt and pepper to taste.

Serve hot, garnished with grated Parmesan cheese if desired.

Nutritional Information: 440 calories, 29g protein, 60g carbohydrates, 12g fat, 8g fiber, 50mg cholesterol, 70mg sodium, 300mg potassium.

Penne with Chickpeas, Spinach, and Tomatoes

INGREDIENTS

- 12 oz penne pasta (whole wheat preferred)
- 2 tablespoons olive oil
- 1 onion, finely chopped
- 2 cloves garlic, minced
- 1 can (15 oz) chickpeas, drained and rinsed
- 1 can (14.5 oz) diced tomatoes, with juice
- 4 cups fresh spinach leaves
- Salt and pepper to taste
- Grated Parmesan cheese for serving (optional)

Prep Time: 10 min　　Cook Time: 20 min　　Serves: 4

DIRECTIONS

Cook the penne according to package instructions until al dente. Drain and set aside.

While the pasta cooks, heat the olive oil in a large skillet over medium heat. Add the onion and garlic, and sauté until the onion is translucent, about 5 minutes.

Add the chickpeas and tomatoes with their juice to the skillet. Bring to a simmer and cook for 10 minutes.

Stir in the spinach and cook until it wilts, about 2-3 minutes. Season with salt and pepper.

Toss the cooked penne with the chickpea and tomato mixture. Serve warm, sprinkled with grated Parmesan cheese if desired.

Nutritional Information: 460 calories, 18g protein, 75g carbohydrates, 9g fat, 12g fiber, 0mg cholesterol, 340mg sodium, 650mg potassium.

Linguine with Garlic Shrimp and Cherry Tomatoes

INGREDIENTS

- 12 oz linguine
- 2 tablespoons olive oil
- 4 cloves garlic, minced
- 1 lb shrimp, peeled and deveined
- 1 pint cherry tomatoes, halved
- 1/4 teaspoon red pepper flakes (optional)
- Salt and black pepper to taste
- 1/4 cup fresh basil, chopped
- 1/4 cup grated Parmesan cheese (optional)

Prep Time: 10 min   Cook Time: 15 min   Serves: 4

DIRECTIONS

Cook the linguine until al dente. Drain and set aside, reserve 1/2 cup of the pasta water. While the pasta cooks, heat the olive oil in a large skillet over medium heat. Add the garlic and sauté until fragrant. Add the shrimp to the skillet and cook for 2-3 minutes per side, or until pink and opaque. Remove the shrimp and set aside. In the same skillet, add the cherry tomatoes and red pepper flakes. Cook for about 5 minutes, until the tomatoes are soft and begin to break down. Season with salt and pepper. Return the shrimp to the skillet along with the cooked linguine. Toss everything together, adding reserved pasta water a little at a time to create a light sauce. Cook for an additional 2 minutes to heat through.

Remove from heat and stir in the fresh basil. Serve with grated Parmesan cheese.

Nutritional Information: 420 calories, 31g protein, 56g carbohydrates, 10g fat, 3g fiber, 175mg cholesterol, 290mg sodium, 470mg potassium.

Vegetable Pasta Primavera with Whole Wheat Fusilli

INGREDIENTS

- 12 oz whole wheat fusilli
- 2 tablespoons olive oil
- 1 small zucchini, sliced
- 1 small yellow squash, sliced
- 1 red bell pepper, julienned
- 1 carrot, julienned
- 1/2 cup cherry tomatoes, halved
- 2 cloves garlic, minced
- 1/2 cup low-sodium vegetable broth
- Salt and pepper to taste
- 1/4 cup grated Parmesan cheese
- 1/4 cup fresh basil, chopped

Prep Time: 15 min   Cook Time: 15 min   Serves: 4

DIRECTIONS

Cook the fusilli according to the package instructions until al dente. Drain and set aside.

Heat olive oil in a large skillet over medium heat. Add garlic and sauté for about 1 minute until fragrant.

Add zucchini, yellow squash, red bell pepper, and carrot to the skillet. Sauté for about 5 minutes until vegetables are tender but still crisp.

Stir in the cherry tomatoes and cook for an additional 2 minutes. Pour in the vegetable broth, and season with salt and pepper. Bring to a simmer.

Toss the cooked fusilli with the vegetables in the skillet. Heat through, making sure everything is well combined.

Serve hot, garnished with grated Parmesan cheese and fresh basil.

Nutritional Information: 350 calories, 14g protein, 65g carbohydrates, 9g fat, 10g fiber, 5mg cholesterol, 200mg sodium, 450mg potassium.

Penne with Sun-dried Tomatoes & Walnuts

INGREDIENTS

- 12 oz whole grain penne pasta
- 1/2 cup sun-dried tomatoes, chopped
- 1/2 cup walnuts, chopped
- 3 tablespoons olive oil
- 2 cloves garlic, minced
- 1/4 teaspoon red pepper flakes (optional)
- 1/2 cup fresh basil leaves, chopped
- Salt and pepper to taste
- Grated Parmesan cheese for serving (optional)

 Prep Time: 15 min

 Cook Time: 15 min

 Serves: 4

DIRECTIONS

Cook the penne until al dente. Drain and set aside, reserve 1 cup of the pasta water. While the pasta cooks, heat the olive oil in a large skillet over medium heat. Add the garlic and red pepper flakes, and sauté until the garlic is fragrant.

Add the sun-dried tomatoes and walnuts to the skillet and cook for another 2-3 minutes, stirring frequently. Add the cooked pasta along with the reserved pasta water. Toss to combine all the ingredients well and heat through, about 2 minutes. Remove from heat and stir in the chopped basil. Season with salt and pepper to taste.

Serve hot, sprinkled with grated Parmesan cheese if desired.

Nutritional Information: 450 calories, 17g protein, 67g carbohydrates, 16g fat, 10g fiber, 0mg cholesterol, 150mg sodium, 420mg potassium.

Greek Pasta Salad with Cucumber, Feta, and Olives

INGREDIENTS

- 8 oz rotini pasta or similar (whole wheat preferred)
- 1 cucumber, diced
- 1 cup cherry tomatoes, halved
- 1/2 red onion, thinly sliced
- 1/2 cup Kalamata olives, pitted and halved
- 3/4 cup feta cheese, crumbled
- 1/4 cup extra virgin olive oil
- 3 tablespoons wine vinegar
- 1 teaspoon dried oregano
- Salt and black pepper
- Fresh parsley, chopped

 Prep Time: 15 min

 Cook Time: 0 min

 Serves: 4

DIRECTIONS

Cook the pasta according to package instructions until al dente. Rinse under cold water to cool and drain well.

In a large bowl, combine the cooled pasta, cucumber, cherry tomatoes, red onion, olives, and feta cheese.

In a small bowl, whisk together the olive oil, red wine vinegar, oregano, salt, and pepper. Pour the dressing over the pasta salad and toss to combine.

Chill the salad in the refrigerator for at least 1 hour to allow flavors to meld.

Serve chilled, garnished with fresh parsley.

Nutritional Information: 380 calories, 12g protein, 42g carbohydrates, 20g fat, 6g fiber, 25mg cholesterol, 580mg sodium, 300mg potassium.

Orzo with Lemon, Asparagus, and Peas

INGREDIENTS

- 1 cup orzo pasta
- 1 bunch asparagus, trimmed and cut into 1-inch pieces
- 1 cup frozen peas, thawed
- Zest and juice of 1 lemon
- 2 tablespoons olive oil
- 1/4 cup grated Parmesan cheese
- Salt and pepper to taste
- Fresh mint or parsley, chopped (optional for garnish)

 Prep Time: 10 min

 Cook Time: 15 min

 Serves: 4

DIRECTIONS

Bring a large pot of salted water to a boil. Add orzo and cook according to package instructions, usually about 8-10 minutes.

Two minutes before the orzo is done, add the asparagus pieces to the boiling water with the orzo. After one minute, add the peas.

Drain the orzo, asparagus, and peas in a colander and return them to the pot.

Stir in the lemon zest, lemon juice, olive oil, and Parmesan cheese. Season with salt and pepper to taste.

Serve warm, garnished with chopped mint or parsley if desired.

Nutritional Information: 280 calories, 10g protein, 42g carbohydrates, 8g fat, 4g fiber, 4mg cholesterol, 180mg sodium, 320mg potassium.

Fusilli with Spinach and Ricotta Sauce

INGREDIENTS

- 12 oz fusilli pasta
- 2 cups fresh spinach leaves, washed and roughly chopped
- 1 cup ricotta cheese
- 1/4 cup grated Parmesan cheese
- 2 cloves garlic, minced
- 2 tablespoons olive oil
- 1/2 teaspoon salt
- 1/4 teaspoon black pepper
- 1/4 cup milk (optional for creamier sauce)
- Fresh basil, chopped (for garnish)

 Prep Time: 10 min

 Cook Time: 15 min

 Serves: 4

DIRECTIONS

Cook the fusilli according to package instructions until al dente. Drain and set aside, reserving 1 cup of pasta water.

In the same pot, heat the olive oil over medium heat. Add the minced garlic and sauté for 1 minute until fragrant.

Add the spinach and cook until it wilts, about 2-3 minutes. Reduce heat to low.

Stir in the ricotta, Parmesan, salt, and pepper. Mix until well combined. If the sauce is too thick, add milk or reserved pasta water to reach desired consistency.

Toss the cooked fusilli with the spinach and ricotta sauce. Heat through, ensuring everything is well mixed and warmed.

Serve immediately, garnished with chopped basil.

Nutritional Information: 410 calories, 18g protein, 54g carbohydrates, 14g fat, 3g fiber, 30mg cholesterol, 420mg sodium, 240mg potassium.

Whole Wheat Spaghetti with Arugula Pesto

INGREDIENTS

- 12 oz whole wheat spaghetti
- 2 cups fresh arugula, washed
- 1/2 cup grated Parmesan cheese
- 1/3 cup pine nuts
- 2 cloves garlic
- 1/2 cup extra virgin olive oil
- Salt and pepper to taste
- Lemon juice (from 1 lemon)

  Prep Time: 10 min

 Cook Time: 10 min

 Serves: 4

DIRECTIONS

Cook the whole wheat spaghetti according to package instructions until al dente. Drain and reserve 1/4 cup of the pasta cooking water.

While the pasta cooks, combine the arugula, Parmesan cheese, pine nuts, and garlic in a food processor. Pulse until coarsely chopped.

With the processor running, slowly add the olive oil and lemon juice until the mixture forms a smooth pesto. Season with salt and pepper to taste.

Toss the cooked spaghetti with the arugula pesto, adding a little reserved pasta water if needed to loosen the sauce.

Serve immediately, optionally garnished with extra Parmesan cheese or a squeeze of lemon.

Nutritional Information: 560 calories, 18g protein, 75g carbohydrates, 24g fat, 10g fiber, 7mg cholesterol, 300mg sodium, 450mg potassium.

Tagliatelle with Eggplant and Tomato Sauce

INGREDIENTS

- 12 oz tagliatelle pasta
- 1 large eggplant, cut into 1/2-inch cubes
- 3 tablespoons olive oil
- 2 cloves garlic, minced
- 1 can (28 oz) crushed tomatoes
- 1 teaspoon dried oregano
- Salt and pepper to taste
- 1/4 cup fresh basil, chopped
- Grated Parmesan cheese for serving

 Prep Time: 15 min

 Cook Time: 30 min

 Serves: 4

DIRECTIONS

Bring a large pot of salted water to a boil. Cook the tagliatelle according to package instructions until al dente. Drain and set aside.

Heat the olive oil in a large skillet over medium heat. Add the eggplant and sauté until it starts to soften and brown, about 10 minutes. Add the garlic and cook for another minute until fragrant.

Pour in the crushed tomatoes and oregano. Season with salt and pepper. Simmer the sauce for about 15 minutes until the eggplant is tender and the sauce has thickened.

Toss the tagliatelle with the eggplant and tomato sauce. Stir in the chopped basil just before serving. Serve hot, topped with grated Parmesan cheese.

Nutritional Information: 450 calories, 14g protein, 67g carbohydrates, 13g fat, 8g fiber, 0mg cholesterol, 320mg sodium, 520mg potassium.

Orzo with Roasted Red Peppers, Spinach, and Feta

INGREDIENTS

- 1 cup orzo pasta
- 1 tablespoon olive oil
- 1 cup roasted red peppers, chopped
- 2 cups fresh spinach leaves
- 1/2 cup feta cheese, crumbled
- Salt and pepper to taste
- Optional: 2 tablespoons fresh basil, chopped for garnish

 Prep Time: 10 min

 Cook Time: 15 min

 Serves: 4

DIRECTIONS

Cook the orzo according to package instructions until al dente. Drain and set aside.

In the same pot, heat the olive oil over medium heat. Add the chopped roasted red peppers and sauté for about 2 minutes.

Add the spinach to the pot and cook until it wilts, about 3-4 minutes.

Stir in the cooked orzo and feta cheese. Mix until well combined and the feta begins to melt slightly. Season with salt and pepper to taste.

Serve warm, garnished with fresh basil if using.

Nutritional Information: 220 calories, 8g protein, 30g carbohydrates, 7g fat, 2g fiber, 15mg cholesterol, 580mg sodium, 180mg potassium.

Linguine with Zucchini, Mint, and Almonds

INGREDIENTS

- 12 oz linguine
- 2 tablespoons olive oil
- 2 medium zucchini, thinly sliced
- 3 cloves garlic, minced
- 1/2 cup slivered almonds
- 1/4 cup fresh mint leaves, chopped
- Salt and pepper to taste
- Grated Parmesan cheese (optional, for serving)

 Prep Time: 10 min

 Cook Time: 15 min

 Serves: 4

DIRECTIONS

Cook the linguine according to package instructions until al dente. Drain, reserving 1/2 cup of the pasta water.

While the pasta cooks, heat the olive oil in a large skillet over medium heat. Add the garlic and sauté for 1 minute until fragrant.

Add the zucchini to the skillet and cook until tender and slightly golden, about 5-7 minutes.

Toss the cooked linguine with the sautéed zucchini in the skillet. Add the reserved pasta water as needed to moisten. Stir in the slivered almonds and fresh mint. Season with salt and pepper to taste.

Serve hot, garnished with grated Parmesan cheese if desired.

Nutritional Information: 430 calories, 14g protein, 60g carbohydrates, 16g fat, 5g fiber, 0mg cholesterol, 70mg sodium, 350mg potassium.

Caponata Pasta Salad with Whole Wheat Penne

INGREDIENTS

- 12 oz whole wheat penne
- 1 medium eggplant, diced into small cubes
- 1 red bell pepper, diced
- 1 zucchini, diced
- 1 onion, chopped
- 3 tablespoons olive oil
- 2 tablespoons wine vinegar
- 1/2 cup pitted and chopped Kalamata olives
- 1/4 cup capers, drained
- 2 tablespoons tomato paste
- 1/4 cup raisins
- Salt and pepper to taste
- Fresh parsley, chopped
- Crumbled feta cheese

Prep Time: 15 min

Cook Time: 20 min

Serves: 4

DIRECTIONS

Preheat your oven to 400°F (200°C). Toss the eggplant, bell pepper, zucchini, and onion with 2 tablespoons of olive oil and spread them on a baking sheet. Roast for about 15 minutes, or until the vegetables are tender and slightly caramelized. Cook the penne until al dente. Drain and set aside to cool. Combine the roasted vegetables with the cooked penne in a large mixing bowl. Add the Kalamata olives, capers, and raisins.

Whisk together the remaining olive oil, wine vinegar, and tomato paste in a small bowl. Season with salt and pepper. Pour the dressing over the pasta salad and toss. Chill in the refrigerator for at least 1 hour to allow the flavors to meld.

Serve the pasta salad garnished with fresh parsley and crumbled feta cheese.

Nutritional Information: 460 calories, 14g protein, 76g carbohydrates, 14g fat, 12g fiber, 0mg cholesterol, 420mg sodium, 470mg potassium.

Whole Wheat Pasta with Clam Sauce

INGREDIENTS

- 12 oz whole wheat spaghetti or linguine
- 2 tablespoons olive oil
- 4 cloves garlic, minced
- 1/2 teaspoon red pepper flakes (optional)
- 2 cans (6.5 ounces each) chopped clams, drained, juice reserved
- 1/2 cup white wine
- 1/2 cup fresh parsley, chopped
- Salt and black pepper to taste
- Lemon wedges for serving

Prep Time: 10 min

Cook Time: 20 min

Serves: 4

DIRECTIONS

Cook the whole wheat pasta until al dente. Drain and set aside.

In a large skillet, heat the olive oil over medium heat. Add the garlic and red pepper flakes, sautéing until the garlic is fragrant, about 1 minute. Add the reserved clam juice and wine. Bring to a simmer and let reduce by half, about 5-7 minutes.

Stir in the chopped clams and cook until heated through, about 3 minutes. Do not overcook to keep clams tender.

Toss the cooked pasta with the clam sauce, adding chopped parsley, and season with salt and pepper. Cook together for an additional 2 minutes to blend the flavors.

Serve hot, garnished with lemon wedges for squeezing over the pasta.

Nutritional Information: 370 calories, 22g protein, 58g carbohydrates, 7g fat, 8g fiber, 30mg cholesterol, 180mg sodium, 200mg potassium.

Baked Penne with Eggplant and Mozzarella

INGREDIENTS

- 12 oz penne pasta
- 1 large eggplant, cut into 1/2-inch cubes
- 3 tablespoons olive oil
- Salt and pepper to taste
- 2 cups marinara sauce
- 1 cup mozzarella cheese, shredded
- 1/2 cup Parmesan cheese, grated
- 1/4 cup fresh basil, chopped
- 2 cloves garlic, minced

Prep Time: 15 min

Cook Time: 45 min

Serves: 4

DIRECTIONS

Preheat the oven to 375°F (190°C). Toss the eggplant cubes with olive oil, salt, and pepper. Spread on a baking sheet and roast until tender and lightly browned, about 25 minutes. While the eggplant is roasting, cook the penne according to package instructions until al dente. Drain and set aside.

In a large mixing bowl, combine the cooked penne, roasted eggplant, marinara sauce, half of the mozzarella, all of the Parmesan, garlic, and half of the basil. Mix well and transfer the pasta mixture to a greased 9x13 inch baking dish. Sprinkle the remaining mozzarella over the top.

Bake in the preheated oven for 20 minutes, or until the cheese is bubbly and golden. Garnish with the remaining basil before serving.

Nutritional Information: 560 calories, 24g protein, 72g carbohydrates, 22g fat, 9g fiber, 35mg cholesterol, 700mg sodium, 500mg potassium.

Meat and Poultry

Stuffed Chicken Breasts with Feta and Spinach

INGREDIENTS

- 4 boneless, skinless chicken breasts
- 1 cup fresh spinach, chopped
- 1/2 cup feta cheese, crumbled
- 1/4 cup sun-dried tomatoes, chopped
- 2 cloves garlic, minced
- 1 tablespoon olive oil
- Salt and pepper to taste

Prep Time: 20 min

Cook Time: 25 min

Serves: 4

DIRECTIONS

Preheat your oven to 375°F (190°C).

Cut a pocket into the side of each chicken breast. In a bowl, combine the spinach, feta, sun-dried tomatoes, and garlic. Stuff this mixture into the pockets of each chicken breast. Season with salt and pepper. Heat the olive oil in an oven-safe skillet over medium-high heat. Sear the chicken on each side until golden, about 3 minutes per side. Transfer the skillet to the oven and bake for 20 minutes.

Nutritional Information: 280 calories, 31g protein, 5g carbohydrates, 15g fat, 1g fiber, 85mg cholesterol, 450mg sodium, 300mg potassium.

Grilled Chicken with Tzatziki Sauce

INGREDIENTS

- 4 skinless chicken breasts
- 2 tablespoons olive oil
- Juice of 1 lemon
- 2 cloves garlic, minced
- 1 teaspoon dried oregano
- Salt and pepper to taste

For the Tzatziki Sauce:

- 1 cup Greek yogurt
- 1 cucumber, seeded and finely grated
- 2 cloves garlic, minced
- 1 tablespoon olive oil
- 1 tablespoon dill, chopped
- Juice of 1/2 lemon
- Salt and pepper to taste

Prep Time: 20 min (plus marinating time) Cook Time: 15 min Serves: 4

DIRECTIONS

Combine olive oil, lemon juice, garlic, oregano, salt, and pepper in a bowl. Add chicken breasts and marinate for at least 30 minutes.

Preheat the grill to medium-high heat. Remove chicken from marinade and grill for 7-8 minutes on each side or until fully cooked.

For the tzatziki sauce, combine Greek yogurt, cucumber, garlic, olive oil, dill, lemon juice, salt, and pepper in a bowl. Mix and refrigerate until ready to serve.

Serve grilled chicken with a generous dollop of tzatziki sauce on the side or over the chicken.

Nutritional Information: 310 calories, 35g protein, 6g carbohydrates, 16g fat, 1g fiber, 85mg cholesterol, 180mg sodium, 350mg potassium.

Turkey Meatballs in Tomato Basil Sauce

INGREDIENTS

- 1 pound ground turkey
- 1/4 cup breadcrumbs
- 1/4 cup grated Parmesan cheese
- 1 large egg
- 2 cloves garlic, minced
- 2 tablespoons fresh parsley, chopped
- Salt and pepper to taste

For the Sauce:

- 2 tablespoons olive oil
- 1 onion, finely chopped
- 2 cloves garlic, minced
- 1 can crushed tomatoes
- 1 teaspoon sugar
- 1/4 cup fresh basil, chopped
- Salt and pepper to taste

Prep Time: 15 min Cook Time: 30 min Serves: 4

DIRECTIONS

In a bowl, combine ground turkey, breadcrumbs, Parmesan, egg, minced garlic, parsley, salt, and pepper. Mix well. Form the mixture into 1-inch meatballs.

Heat a non-stick skillet over medium heat and cook the meatballs until browned on all sides, about 10 minutes. Remove from skillet and set aside.

In the same skillet, add olive oil and sauté onion and garlic until translucent. Stir in crushed tomatoes, sugar, and season with salt and pepper. Bring to a simmer.

Add the meatballs back to the skillet with the tomato sauce. Cover and let simmer for 20 minutes, until meatballs are cooked through.

Stir in chopped basil just before serving.

Serve the meatballs and sauce over cooked whole wheat spaghetti or your preferred pasta, or enjoy them on their own.

Nutritional Information: 350 calories, 28g protein, 22g carbohydrates, 17g fat, 4g fiber, 100mg cholesterol, 470mg sodium, 700mg potassium.

Stuffed Bell Peppers with Ground Beef and Herbs

INGREDIENTS

- 4 large bell peppers, tops cut off and seeds removed
- 1 tablespoon olive oil
- 1 small onion, chopped
- 2 cloves garlic, minced
- 1-pound lean ground beef
- 1 teaspoon salt
- 1/2 teaspoon black pepper
- 1 teaspoon dried oregano
- 1 teaspoon dried basil
- 1/2 cup cooked brown rice
- 1 cup tomato sauce
- 1/4 cup grated Parmesan cheese
- 1/4 cup fresh parsley, chopped

Prep Time: 15 min

Cook Time: 45 min

Serves: 4

DIRECTIONS

Preheat oven to 375°F (190°C). Prepare a baking dish by lightly greasing it or lining it with parchment paper.

In a skillet over medium heat, add olive oil, onion, and garlic. Sauté until onions are translucent, about 5 minutes. Add ground beef. Cook, breaking up the meat with a spoon, until browned and cooked through. Drain any excess fat. Stir in salt, pepper, oregano, basil, cooked rice, and half of the tomato sauce. Mix well.

Stuff each bell pepper with the beef and rice mixture. Place stuffed peppers upright in the baking dish. Spoon the remaining tomato sauce over the tops of the peppers. Cover with foil and bake for 35 minutes. Remove foil, sprinkle each pepper with Parmesan cheese, and bake uncovered for 10 minutes.

Garnish with fresh parsley before serving.

Nutritional Information: 330 calories, 26g protein, 28g carbohydrates, 15g fat, 5g fiber, 70mg cholesterol, 890mg sodium, 650mg potassium.

Chicken Souvlaki with Lemon and Oregano

INGREDIENTS

- 1 1/2 pounds chicken breast, cut into 1-inch cubes
- 3 tablespoons olive oil
- Juice of 1 lemon
- 3 cloves garlic, minced
- 2 teaspoons dried oregano
- Salt and pepper to taste
- Lemon wedges, for serving
- Fresh oregano, for garnish (optional)

Prep Time: 15 min
(plus marinating time)

Cook Time: 10 min

Serves: 4

DIRECTIONS

In a bowl, combine olive oil, lemon juice, garlic, oregano, salt, and pepper. Add the chicken cubes and toss to coat evenly. Cover and refrigerate for at least 1 hour, preferably 2-3 hours, to marinate.

Preheat an outdoor grill or a grill pan on the stove over medium-high heat. Thread the marinated chicken cubes onto skewers. Grill the skewers for 8-10 minutes, turning occasionally, until the chicken is golden on all sides and cooked through.

Serve hot, garnished with lemon wedges and fresh oregano if using. Accompany with a side of tzatziki sauce or a fresh Greek salad for a complete meal.

Nutritional Information: 290 calories, 35g protein, 3g carbohydrates, 16g fat, 1g fiber, 85mg cholesterol, 180mg sodium, 300mg potassium.

Moroccan Lamb Tagine with Prunes and Almonds

INGREDIENTS

- 1.5 pounds lamb shoulder, cut into 1-inch cubes
- 2 tablespoons olive oil
- 1 large onion, chopped
- 2 cloves garlic, minced
- 1 teaspoon ground cinnamon
- 1 teaspoon ground cumin
- 1/2 teaspoon ground ginger
- 1/2 teaspoon turmeric
- Salt and pepper to taste
- 2 cups beef or lamb broth
- 1/2 cup prunes, pitted
- 1/2 cup blanched almonds
- 1 tablespoon honey
- 2 tablespoons sesame seeds
- Fresh cilantro, chopped

Prep Time: 20 min

Cook Time: 120 minutes

Serves: 4

DIRECTIONS

Heat the olive oil in a large tagine or heavy-bottomed pot over medium-high heat. Add the lamb pieces and brown on all sides. Remove the lamb and set aside.

In the same pot, add the onion and garlic, cooking until the onion is translucent. Stir in the cinnamon, cumin, ginger, turmeric, salt, and pepper. Cook for another 2 minutes until fragrant.

Return the lamb to the pot along with the broth. Bring to a boil, then reduce the heat to low, cover, and simmer for 1.5 hours, or until the lamb is tender.

Add the prunes, almonds, and honey to the pot. Continue to simmer, uncovered, for another 30 minutes, allowing the sauce to thicken slightly.

Toast the sesame seeds in a dry skillet until golden brown. Sprinkle the toasted sesame seeds and chopped cilantro over the tagine just before serving.

Nutritional Information: 480 calories, 38g protein, 30g carbohydrates, 24g fat, 5g fiber, 105mg cholesterol, 620mg sodium, 740mg potassium.

Pork Tenderloin with Herbs and Garlic

INGREDIENTS

- 1 pork tenderloin (about 1 to 1.5 pounds)
- 3 tablespoons olive oil
- 4 cloves garlic, minced
- 2 tablespoons fresh rosemary, chopped
- 2 tablespoons fresh thyme, chopped
- Salt and pepper to taste

Prep Time: 15 min

Cook Time: 25 min

Serves: 4

DIRECTIONS

Preheat your oven to 375°F (190°C).

In a small bowl, combine olive oil, garlic, rosemary, thyme, salt, and pepper to create a marinade. Rub the marinade all over the pork tenderloin.

Heat a skillet over medium-high heat. Once hot, add the pork tenderloin and sear it on all sides until golden brown, about 2-3 minutes per side.

Transfer the seared pork to a baking dish and place it in the preheated oven. Roast for 20-25 minutes.

Remove the pork from the oven and let it rest for 5 minutes before slicing. Serve the sliced pork with a side of vegetables or a salad for a complete meal.

Nutritional Information: 230 calories, 24g protein, 2g carbohydrates, 14g fat, 0g fiber, 70mg cholesterol, 65mg sodium, 360mg potassium.

Roasted Chicken with Mediterranean Herb Rub

INGREDIENTS

- 1 whole chicken (approximately 4 pounds)
- 2 tablespoons olive oil
- 2 teaspoons dried oregano
- 2 teaspoons dried thyme
- 1 teaspoon dried rosemary
- 2 cloves garlic, minced
- 1 lemon, zested and juiced
- Salt and pepper to taste

Prep Time: 15 min

Cook Time: 45 min

Serves: 4

DIRECTIONS

Preheat your oven to 400°F (200°C).

In a small bowl, mix together the olive oil, oregano, thyme, rosemary, garlic, lemon zest, and lemon juice to create the herb rub. Season with salt and pepper.

Rinse the chicken under cold water and pat dry with paper towels. Rub the herb mixture all over the chicken, making sure to coat both the outside and under the skin for added flavor.

Place the chicken in a roasting pan. If desired, you can add vegetables like carrots, potatoes, and onions around the chicken for a complete meal. Roast in the preheated oven for about 45 minutes, or until the chicken is golden brown and a meat thermometer inserted into the thickest part of the thigh reads 165°F (75°C).

Let the chicken rest for 10 minutes after removing it from the oven. This allows the juices to redistribute throughout the meat. Carve and serve warm.

Nutritional Information: 370 calories, 35g protein, 3g carbohydrates, 23g fat, 1g fiber, 95mg cholesterol, 340mg sodium, 360mg potassium.

Turkish Chicken Kebabs with Red Pepper

INGREDIENTS

- 1-pound boneless, skinless chicken breasts
- 2 large red bell peppers
- 1 large onion
- 3 tablespoons olive oil
- 2 tablespoons lemon juice
- 2 cloves garlic, minced
- 2 teaspoons paprika
- 1 teaspoon ground cumin
- 1/2 teaspoon ground coriander
- 1/2 teaspoon salt
- 1/4 teaspoon black pepper

Prep Time: 20 min

Cook Time: 15 min

Serves: 4

DIRECTIONS

Cut the chicken breasts, bell peppers and onion into 1-inch pieces.

Combine the olive oil, lemon juice, minced garlic, paprika, cumin, coriander, salt, and pepper in a large bowl. Add the chicken pieces and toss to coat evenly. Let marinate in the refrigerator for at least 15 minutes, or up to 2 hours for more flavor.

Preheat the grill to medium-high heat. Thread the marinated chicken, bell peppers, and onions alternately onto skewers.

Grill the skewers, turning occasionally, until the chicken is cooked through and the vegetables are tender and slightly charred, about 10-15 minutes.

Nutritional Information: 290 calories, 26g protein, 10g carbohydrates, 16g fat, 3g fiber, 65mg cholesterol, 350mg sodium, 500mg potassium.

Greek Moussaka with Ground Lamb

INGREDIENTS

- 2 large eggplants
- 4 tablespoons olive oil
- 1 pound ground lamb
- 1 large onion, chopped
- 3 cloves garlic, minced
- 1 can crushed tomatoes
- 1/4 cup red wine
- 1 teaspoon cinnamon
- 1/2 teaspoon allspice
- 2 tablespoons fresh parsley

For the Béchamel Sauce:
- 4 tablespoons butter
- 1/4 cup all-purpose flour
- 2 cups milk
- 1/4 teaspoon nutmeg
- 1/2 cup Parmesan cheese
- 2 egg yolks

Prep Time: 30 min   Cook Time: 70 min   Serves: 6

DIRECTIONS

Slice the eggplants into 1/4-inch rounds. Brush slices with 2 tablespoons olive oil and season with salt. Arrange on baking sheets and bake at 425°F for 20 minutes, until lightly browned.

Heat remaining olive oil in a skillet over medium heat. Sauté onion and garlic until soft. Add lamb, breaking it up with a spoon, and brown it. Stir in crushed tomatoes, wine, cinnamon, allspice, salt, and pepper. Simmer for 20 minutes. Chop the parsley and stir it in.

Melt butter in a saucepan. Whisk in flour until smooth. Gradually add milk, whisking continuously until thickened. Remove from heat. Stir in nutmeg and Parmesan. Slowly whisk in egg yolks until smooth.

In a greased baking dish, layer half the eggplant, top with all the lamb mixture, then remaining eggplant. Pour béchamel sauce over the top. Bake at 350°F for 45 minutes until golden.

Nutritional Information: 510 calories, 23g protein, 35g carbohydrates, 32g fat, 9g fiber, 145mg cholesterol, 410mg sodium, 800mg potassium.

Italian Beef Braciole Stuffed with Herbs and Cheese

INGREDIENTS

- 4 thin slices top round beef (about 1 1/2 pounds)
- 4 ounces mozzarella cheese, thinly sliced
- 1/4 cup grated Parmesan cheese
- 1/4 cup fresh parsley, chopped
- 2 cloves garlic, minced
- 1/2 teaspoon salt
- 1/4 teaspoon black pepper
- 2 tablespoons olive oil
- 2 cups marinara sauce
- Kitchen twine or toothpicks for securing

Prep Time: 30 min   Cook Time: 90 min   Serves: 4

DIRECTIONS

Lay the beef slices flat on a work surface. Sprinkle with salt, pepper, parsley, and minced garlic. Arrange mozzarella slices on top of each beef slice, then sprinkle with Parmesan cheese. Roll up each beef slice, securing the rolls with kitchen twine or toothpicks. Heat olive oil in a large skillet over medium-high heat. Brown the beef rolls on all sides, about 8 minutes total. Add the marinara sauce to the skillet, cover, and reduce the heat to low. Simmer the beef braciole in the sauce for 70-80 minutes. Occasionally baste the rolls with the sauce during cooking. Remove the twine or toothpicks before serving.

Serve with extra sauce spooned over the top.

Nutritional Information: 410 calories, 44g protein, 8g carbohydrates, 22g fat, 2g fiber, 115mg cholesterol, 900mg sodium, 650mg potassium.

Chicken Cacciatore with Olives and Peppers

INGREDIENTS

- 4 boneless, skinless chicken breasts
- 1 teaspoon salt
- 1/2 teaspoon black pepper
- 2 tablespoons olive oil
- 1 large onion, thinly sliced
- 2 bell peppers (1 red, 1 green), thinly sliced
- 3 cloves garlic, minced
- 1 cup sliced mushrooms
- 1/2 cup pitted kalamata olives, halved
- 1 can (14.5 ounces) diced tomatoes
- 1 teaspoon dried oregano
- 1 teaspoon dried basil
- 1/2 cup chicken broth

Prep Time: 15 min

Cook Time: 45 min

Serves: 4

DIRECTIONS

Season the chicken breasts with salt and pepper. Heat olive oil in a large skillet over medium-high heat. Add the chicken and brown on both sides, about 3-4 minutes per side. Remove the chicken from the skillet and set aside.

In the same skillet, add the onion, bell peppers, garlic, and mushrooms. Sauté until the vegetables are softened, about 5-7 minutes.

Stir in the olives, diced tomatoes, oregano, basil, and chicken broth. Bring to a simmer.

Return the chicken to the skillet, spooning the sauce and vegetables over the chicken. Cover and simmer for 25 minutes until the chicken is cooked and tender. Adjust seasoning with additional salt and pepper if needed before serving.

Nutritional Information: 320 calories, 35g protein, 15g carbohydrates, 12g fat, 4g fiber, 85mg cholesterol, 890mg sodium, 600mg potassium.

Spicy Moroccan Chicken with Preserved Lemons

INGREDIENTS

- 4 boneless, skinless chicken breasts
- 1 tablespoon olive oil
- 1 large onion, chopped
- 2 cloves garlic, minced
- 2 teaspoons ground cumin
- 1 teaspoon cinnamon
- 1 teaspoon paprika
- 1/2 teaspoon cayenne pepper
- 1 cup chicken broth
- 1/2 cup preserved lemons, thinly sliced
- 1/2 cup green olives, pitted
- 1/4 cup cilantro, chopped
- Salt and black pepper

Prep Time: 15 min

Cook Time: 40 min

Serves: 4

DIRECTIONS

Heat olive oil in a large skillet over medium-high heat. Season chicken breasts with salt and pepper, and brown them on each side for about 3-4 minutes. Remove the chicken from the skillet and set aside.

In the same skillet, add the onion and garlic, sautéing until the onion is translucent, about 5 minutes. Stir in the cumin, cinnamon, paprika, and cayenne pepper, cooking for another minute until fragrant.

Return the chicken to the skillet, add chicken broth, preserved lemons, and olives. Bring to a simmer, then cover and reduce heat to low. Cook for 25-30 minutes, or until the chicken is cooked through and tender.

Remove from heat and stir in fresh cilantro just before serving.

Nutritional Information: 265 calories, 27g protein, 9g carbohydrates, 12g fat, 2g fiber, 75mg cholesterol, 870mg sodium, 350mg potassium.

Lamb Gyros with Cucumber Yogurt Sauce

INGREDIENTS

- 1 pound ground lamb
- 1 teaspoon garlic powder
- 1 teaspoon onion powder
- 1 teaspoon dried oregano
- 1/2 teaspoon ground cumin
- 1/2 teaspoon paprika
- 4 pita breads
- 1 tomato, sliced
- 1 red onion, thinly sliced
  Cucumber Yogurt Sauce:
- 1 cup plain Greek yogurt
- 1/2 cucumber, grated and excess water squeezed out
- 1 clove garlic, minced
- 2 tablespoons lemon juice
- 1 tablespoon olive oil

 Prep Time: 20 min

 Cook Time: 10 min

Serves: 4

DIRECTIONS

In a bowl, mix together the ground lamb, garlic powder, onion powder, oregano, cumin, paprika, salt, and pepper. Form into thin patties or shape like a sausage directly on skewers.

Preheat a grill or skillet over medium-high heat. Cook the lamb for about 4-5 minutes on each side, or until fully cooked and slightly charred.

For the cucumber yogurt sauce, combine Greek yogurt, grated cucumber, minced garlic, lemon juice, olive oil, salt, and pepper in a bowl. Mix well until smooth.

Warm the pita breads on the grill or in a dry skillet. Place the cooked lamb in the center of each pita, top with tomato slices, red onion, and a generous dollop of cucumber yogurt sauce.

Fold the pita around the fillings and serve immediately.

Nutritional Information: 510 calories, 31g protein, 38g carbohydrates, 27g fat, 3g fiber, 85mg cholesterol, 590mg sodium, 510mg potassium.

Braised Chicken with Capers and Olives

INGREDIENTS

- 4 boneless, skinless chicken breasts
- 2 tablespoons olive oil
- 1 onion, finely chopped
- 3 cloves garlic, minced
- 1 cup chicken broth
- 1/2 cup white wine
- 1 cup cherry tomatoes
- 1/4 cup capers, rinsed
- 1/4 cup kalamata olives, pitted and halved
- 1 lemon, sliced
- 1 tablespoon thyme leaves
- Salt and pepper to taste

 Prep Time: 15 min

 Cook Time: 45 min

 Serves: 4

DIRECTIONS

Season the chicken breasts with salt and pepper. Heat olive oil in a large skillet over medium-high heat. Add the chicken and sear until golden brown on both sides, about 3-4 minutes per side. Remove chicken and set aside.

In the same skillet, add the onion and garlic, and cook until the onion is translucent, about 5 minutes. Deglaze the pan with white wine, scraping up any browned bits from the bottom. Return the chicken to the skillet. Add broth, cherry tomatoes, capers, olives, and lemon slices. Bring to a simmer, cover and cook for 30 minutes on low heat, or until the chicken is tender and cooked through.

Uncover, increase heat to medium, and cook for an additional 10 minutes to reduce the sauce slightly. Sprinkle with fresh thyme before serving.

Nutritional Information: 290 calories, 26g protein, 9g carbohydrates, 15g fat, 2g fiber, 75mg cholesterol, 490mg sodium, 300mg potassium.

Chicken Shawarma with Yogurt Sauce

INGREDIENTS

- 1-pound boneless, skinless chicken thighs
- 2 tablespoons olive oil
- 1 teaspoon ground cumin
- 1 teaspoon paprika
- 1/2 teaspoon turmeric
- 1/4 teaspoon cinnamon
- 1/4 teaspoon ground cloves
- 4 pita breads

  Yogurt Sauce:
- 1 cup plain Greek yogurt
- 2 tablespoons lemon juice
- 1 clove garlic, minced
- 1 tablespoon dill, chopped

 Prep Time: 20 min

 Cook Time: 10 min

Serves: 4

DIRECTIONS

In a large bowl, mix olive oil, cumin, paprika, turmeric, cinnamon, cloves, salt, and pepper. Add the chicken thighs and coat well with the marinade. Let it marinate for at least 10 minutes, or up to 4 hours. Heat a grill or skillet over medium-high heat. Cook the chicken about 5 minutes per side until it is cooked through.

For the yogurt sauce, combine Greek yogurt, lemon juice, minced garlic, and dill in a small bowl. Season with salt and pepper to taste and mix well.

Warm the pita breads on the grill or in a skillet for about 30 seconds per side.

Slice the cooked chicken and serve it wrapped in warm pita with yogurt sauce.

Nutritional Information: 350 calories, 28g protein, 27g carbohydrates, 15g fat, 2g fiber, 95mg cholesterol, 350mg sodium, 300mg potassium.

Chicken and Artichoke Paella

INGREDIENTS

- 1 pound boneless, skinless chicken thighs, cut into pieces
- 1 tablespoon olive oil
- 1 onion, chopped
- 2 cloves garlic, minced
- 1 red bell pepper, sliced
- 1 1/2 cups Arborio rice
- 4 cups chicken broth
- 1 cup canned artichoke hearts, drained and quartered
- 1/2 cup frozen peas
- 1 teaspoon smoked paprika
- 1/2 teaspoon saffron
- Salt and pepper to taste
- Lemon wedges
- Fresh parsley, chopped

 Prep Time: 15 min

 Cook Time: 40 min

Serves: 4

DIRECTIONS

Heat olive oil in a large skillet or paella pan over medium-high heat. Add the chicken pieces and brown all sides, about 5-7 minutes. Remove chicken and set aside.

In the same pan, add the onion, garlic, and red bell pepper. Sauté until the onion is translucent, about 5 minutes.

Stir in the Arborio rice and cook for 1-2 minutes until the grains are well-coated and slightly toasted. Add the chicken broth, saffron, and smoked paprika. Bring to a boil, then reduce the heat to maintain a gentle simmer.

Add the artichoke hearts and the previously browned chicken back to the pan. Cover and cook for 25 minutes, or until the rice is tender and the liquid is mostly absorbed.

Stir in the peas and cook for an additional 5 minutes. Season with salt and pepper to taste. Serve the paella with lemon wedges and sprinkle with fresh parsley.

Nutritional Information: 430 calories, 28g protein, 59g carbohydrates, 10g fat, 4g fiber, 110mg cholesterol, 590mg sodium, 370mg potassium.

Herb-Roasted Turkey Breast with Garlic

INGREDIENTS

- 2 pounds turkey breast, bone-in, skin-on
- 4 cloves garlic, minced
- 2 tablespoons olive oil
- 1 tablespoon fresh rosemary, chopped
- 1 tablespoon fresh thyme, chopped
- 1 teaspoon salt
- 1/2 teaspoon black pepper
- 1 lemon, halved

Prep Time: 15 min

Cook Time: 90 min

Serves: 4

DIRECTIONS

Preheat your oven to 350°F (175°C). In a small bowl, mix together the olive oil, garlic, rosemary, thyme, salt, and pepper. Pat the turkey breast dry with paper towels. Rub the herb mixture all over the turkey breast, under the skin, and inside. Place the turkey breast in a roasting pan. Squeeze the lemon halves over the turkey and place the squeezed lemon halves into the pan around the turkey.

Roast the turkey in the preheated oven for about 1 hour and 30 minutes, or until the internal temperature reaches 165°F (74°C). Baste occasionally with the pan juices.

Let the turkey rest for 10 minutes before slicing. Serve with the roasted lemon as a garnish.

Nutritional Information: 340 calories, 53g protein, 2g carbohydrates, 14g fat, 1g fiber, 125mg cholesterol, 670mg sodium, 490mg potassium.

Chicken Gyros with Cucumber Salsa and Tsatsiki

INGREDIENTS

- 1-pound boneless, skinless chicken thighs, thinly sliced
- 2 tablespoons olive oil
- 1 teaspoon dried oregano
- 1/2 teaspoon garlic powder
- Salt and pepper to taste
- 4 pita breads
  Cucumber Salsa:
- 1 large cucumber, diced
- 1/2 red onion, chopped
- 1 tomato, diced
- 1 tablespoon chopped parsley
- Juice of 1 lemon
- Salt and pepper to taste
- Tsatsiki Sauce (page 36)

Prep Time: 20 min

Cook Time: 10 min

Serves: 4

DIRECTIONS

In a mixing bowl, combine chicken thighs with olive oil, oregano, garlic powder, salt, and pepper. Let marinate for at least 10 minutes.

Heat a skillet over medium-high heat. Add the chicken and cook until golden and cooked through, about 5-7 minutes per side.

For the cucumber salsa, mix cucumber, red onion, tomato, parsley, and lemon juice in a bowl. Season with salt and pepper to taste. Set aside.

Warm the pita breads in the oven or on a skillet. Assemble the gyros by placing some chicken in each pita, topped with cucumber salsa and a generous dollop of tsatsiki sauce.

Nutritional Information: 440 calories, 32g protein, 38g carbohydrates, 19g fat, 4g fiber, 125mg cholesterol, 470mg sodium, 630mg potassium.

Moroccan Spiced Chicken with Dried Apricots

INGREDIENTS

- 4 boneless, skinless chicken breasts
- 1 tablespoon olive oil
- 1 large onion, thinly sliced
- 2 cloves garlic, minced
- 1 teaspoon ground cumin
- 1 teaspoon ground cinnamon
- 1/2 teaspoon ground ginger
- 1/2 teaspoon turmeric
- 1/2 cup dried apricots, sliced
- 1/2 cup chicken broth
- 1/4 cup chopped fresh cilantro
- Salt and pepper to taste

Prep Time: 15 min   Cook Time: 30 min   Serves: 4

DIRECTIONS

Heat the olive oil in a large skillet over medium heat. Season the chicken breasts with salt and pepper, and sear each side until golden brown, about 3-4 minutes per side. Remove chicken from the skillet and set aside.

In the same skillet, add the onion and garlic, cooking until the onion becomes translucent, about 5 minutes. Stir in the cumin, cinnamon, ginger, and turmeric, cooking for another minute until fragrant.

Return the chicken to the skillet, adding the dried apricots and chicken broth. Bring to a simmer, then cover and reduce heat to low. Cook for 20 minutes, or until the chicken is cooked through and tender.

Sprinkle with fresh cilantro just before serving.

Nutritional Information: 280 calories, 27g protein, 20g carbohydrates, 9g fat, 3g fiber, 75mg cholesterol, 270mg sodium, 370mg potassium.

Grilled Chicken with Mediterranean Salsa

INGREDIENTS

- 4 boneless, skinless chicken breasts
- 2 tablespoons olive oil
- Salt and pepper to taste
- 1 teaspoon dried oregano

Mediterranean Salsa:

- 1 cup cherry tomatoes, halved
- 1/2 cup cucumber, diced
- 1/4 cup red onion, chopped
- 1/4 cup kalamata olives, sliced
- 1/4 cup feta cheese, crumbled
- 2 tablespoons fresh basil, chopped
- Juice of 1 lemon
- Salt and pepper to taste

Prep Time: 15 min   Cook Time: 10 min   Serves: 4

DIRECTIONS

Preheat the grill to medium-high heat. Brush the chicken breasts with olive oil and season with salt, pepper, and oregano.

Grill the chicken for about 5 minutes on each side or until fully cooked and the internal temperature reaches 165°F.

While the chicken is grilling, combine the cherry tomatoes, cucumber, red onion, kalamata olives, feta cheese, basil, and lemon juice in a bowl. Season with salt and pepper to taste, and mix well to create the Mediterranean salsa.

Serve the grilled chicken topped with a generous amount of Mediterranean salsa.

Nutritional Information: 290 calories, 31g protein, 9g carbohydrates, 14g fat, 2g fiber, 85mg cholesterol, 420mg sodium, 290mg potassium.

Seafood and Fish

Mediterranean Baked Fish with Tomatoes and Capers

INGREDIENTS

- 4 white fish fillets (such as cod, tilapia, or halibut)
- 2 tablespoons olive oil
- 2 cups cherry tomatoes, halved
- 1/4 cup capers, drained
- 3 cloves garlic, minced
- 1/2 cup Kalamata olives, pitted and sliced
- 1 lemon, sliced into rounds
- 1/4 cup fresh parsley, chopped
- Salt and pepper to taste

 Prep Time: 10 min

 Cook Time: 20 min

 Serves: 4

DIRECTIONS

Preheat the oven to 400°F (200°C). Grease a baking dish with 1 tablespoon of olive oil.

Arrange the fish fillets in the prepared baking dish. Season with salt and pepper.

In a bowl, combine the cherry tomatoes, capers, minced garlic, and olives with the remaining olive oil. Toss to coat.

Scatter the tomato mixture around and over the fish. Top each fillet with a slice or two of lemon.

Bake in the preheated oven for about 15-20 minutes, or until the fish flakes easily with a fork.

Garnish with fresh parsley before serving.

Nutritional Information: 220 calories, 23g protein, 8g carbohydrates, 10g fat, 2g fiber, 55mg cholesterol, 580mg sodium, 450mg potassium.

Grilled Salmon with Olive Tapenade

INGREDIENTS

- 4 salmon fillets (about 6 ounces each)
- 2 tablespoons olive oil
- Salt and pepper to taste
- 1 cup pitted Kalamata olives
- 2 cloves garlic, minced
- 1 tablespoon capers, rinsed
- 1 tablespoon fresh lemon juice
- 2 teaspoons chopped fresh rosemary
- 1/4 cup chopped fresh parsley

 Prep Time: 15 min

 Cook Time: 10 min

 Serves: 4

DIRECTIONS

Preheat your grill to medium-high heat. Brush the salmon fillets with olive oil and season them with salt and pepper.

Grill the salmon, skin side down, without flipping, until cooked through, about 6-8 minutes, depending on thickness.

While the salmon is grilling, make the olive tapenade. In a food processor, combine the Kalamata olives, garlic, capers, lemon juice, and rosemary. Pulse until the mixture is finely chopped but not pureed.

Serve the grilled salmon fillets topped with a generous spoonful of olive tapenade and garnish with chopped parsley.

Nutritional Information: 320 calories, 23g protein, 3g carbohydrates, 24g fat, 1g fiber, 60mg cholesterol, 560mg sodium, 400mg potassium.

Grilled Sardines with Lemon and Herbs

INGREDIENTS

- 16 fresh sardines, cleaned and gutted
- 2 tablespoons olive oil
- 2 lemons, one sliced and one juiced
- 1/4 cup chopped fresh parsley
- 1 tablespoon chopped fresh oregano
- Salt and pepper to taste

Prep Time: 10 min

Cook Time: 6 min

Serves: 4

DIRECTIONS

Preheat your grill to medium-high heat. Rinse the sardines under cold water and pat them dry with paper towels.

In a small bowl, mix together olive oil, lemon juice, parsley, oregano, salt, and pepper. Brush this mixture over both sides of the sardines.

Place the sardines on the grill and cook for about 3 minutes on each side, or until the skin is crispy and the fish is cooked through.

Serve the grilled sardines with additional lemon slices for squeezing over the top.

Nutritional Information: 220 calories, 24g protein, 1g carbohydrates, 14g fat, 0g fiber, 85mg cholesterol, 340mg sodium, 300mg potassium.

Pan-Seared Tuna with Mediterranean Salsa

INGREDIENTS

- 4 tuna steaks (about 6 ounces each)
- 2 tablespoons olive oil
- Salt and pepper to taste
  Mediterranean Salsa:
- 1 cup cherry tomatoes, halved
- 1/2 cup pitted Kalamata olives, chopped
- 1/4 cup red onion, finely chopped
- 1/4 cup fresh basil, chopped
- 2 tablespoons capers, rinsed
- Juice of 1 lemon
- Salt and pepper to taste

Prep Time: 15 min

Cook Time: 6 min

Serves: 4

DIRECTIONS

For the salsa, in a bowl combine cherry tomatoes, Kalamata olives, red onion, basil, capers, and lemon juice. Season with salt and pepper to taste and set aside to let the flavors meld.

Heat olive oil in a large skillet over medium-high heat. Season tuna steaks with salt and pepper on both sides.

Place the tuna in the skillet and sear for about 3 minutes on each side for medium-rare, or adjust the cooking time to your preference.

Remove the tuna from the skillet and let it rest for a few minutes before serving.

Serve the tuna steaks topped with the Mediterranean salsa.

Nutritional Information: 280 calories, 27g protein, 5g carbohydrates, 16g fat, 2g fiber, 50mg cholesterol, 380mg sodium, 500mg potassium.

Grilled Mackerel with Salad Greens

INGREDIENTS

- 4 mackerel fillets
- 2 tablespoons olive oil
- Salt and pepper to taste
- Juice of 1 lemon

Salad Greens:

- 4 cups mixed salad greens
- 1/2 cup cherry tomatoes, halved
- 1/4 cup red onion, thinly sliced
- 2 tablespoons balsamic vinegar
- 1 tablespoon extra-virgin olive oil
- Salt and pepper to taste

Prep Time: 10 min

Cook Time: 10 min

Serves: 4

DIRECTIONS

Preheat your grill to medium-high heat. Brush the mackerel fillets with olive oil and season them with salt, pepper, and lemon juice.

Grill the mackerel fillets, skin-side down, for about 5 minutes, then flip and grill for another 5 minutes or until the fish is cooked through and the skin is crispy.

While the mackerel is grilling, prepare the salad by tossing the mixed greens, cherry tomatoes, and red onion with balsamic vinegar, olive oil, salt, and pepper in a large bowl.

Serve the grilled mackerel on a bed of the salad greens mixture.

Nutritional Information: 290 calories, 23g protein, 5g carbohydrates, 20g fat, 2g fiber, 75mg cholesterol, 200mg sodium, 600mg potassium.

Fish Stew with Tomatoes and Fennel

INGREDIENTS

- 1 pound firm white fish (such as cod or halibut), cut into chunks
- 2 tablespoons olive oil
- 1 fennel bulb, thinly sliced
- 1 onion, chopped
- 2 cloves garlic, minced
- 1 teaspoon dried thyme
- 1/4 teaspoon red pepper flakes (optional)
- 1 can (28 ounces) diced tomatoes
- 1 cup fish or vegetable broth
- Salt and pepper to taste
- Juice of 1 lemon
- 1/4 cup chopped fresh parsley

Prep Time: 15 min

Cook Time: 30 min

Serves: 4

DIRECTIONS

Heat olive oil in a large pot over medium heat. Add the sliced fennel and chopped onion, and sauté until the vegetables are softened, about 5 minutes. Add garlic, thyme, and red pepper flakes; cook for an additional minute until fragrant.

Pour in the diced tomatoes and broth. Bring to a simmer, then reduce the heat and let it cook gently for about 20 minutes to allow the flavors to blend.

Add the fish chunks to the pot, season with salt and pepper, and simmer gently until the fish is cooked through, about 10 minutes.

Stir in the lemon juice and chopped parsley just before serving.

Nutritional Information: 230 calories, 23g protein, 14g carbohydrates, 9g fat, 4g fiber, 45mg cholesterol, 420mg sodium, 750mg potassium.

Grilled Sea Bass with Garlic and Herbs

INGREDIENTS

- 4 sea bass fillets (about 6 ounces each)
- 3 tablespoons olive oil
- 4 cloves garlic, minced
- 2 tablespoons fresh parsley, chopped
- 1 tablespoon fresh rosemary, chopped
- 1 tablespoon fresh thyme, chopped
- Juice of 1 lemon
- Salt and pepper to taste

 Prep Time: 15 min

 Cook Time: 10 min

 Serves: 4

DIRECTIONS

In a small bowl, mix together olive oil, minced garlic, chopped parsley, rosemary, thyme, lemon juice, salt, and pepper.

Brush the sea bass fillets with the herb and garlic mixture, ensuring both sides are well coated. Let marinate for about 10 minutes.

Preheat the grill to medium-high heat. Place the fillets on the grill, skin side down, and cook for about 5 minutes. Carefully flip the fillets and grill for another 5 minutes, or until the fish flakes easily with a fork and is opaque throughout.

Serve immediately, with additional lemon wedges if desired.

Nutritional Information: 230 calories, 23g protein, 1g carbohydrates, 15g fat, 0g fiber, 60mg cholesterol, 85mg sodium, 450mg potassium.

Baked Salmon with Lemon and Dill

INGREDIENTS

- 4 salmon fillets (about 6 ounces each)
- 2 tablespoons olive oil
- Juice of 1 lemon, plus additional lemon slices for garnish
- 2 tablespoons fresh dill, chopped
- Salt and pepper to taste

 Prep Time: 10 min

 Cook Time: 15 min

 Serves: 4

DIRECTIONS

Preheat the oven to 400°F (200°C). Line a baking sheet with parchment paper for easy cleanup.

Place the salmon fillets on the prepared baking sheet. Drizzle with olive oil and lemon juice, then season with salt and pepper.

Sprinkle chopped dill over the salmon fillets. Arrange a few lemon slices on and around the salmon for added flavor and presentation.

Bake in the preheated oven for about 15 minutes, or until the salmon is cooked through and flakes easily with a fork.

Serve hot, garnished with additional fresh dill and lemon slices if desired.

Nutritional Information: 280 calories, 23g protein, 1g carbohydrates, 20g fat, 0g fiber, 60mg cholesterol, 75mg sodium, 500mg potassium.

Seafood Paella

INGREDIENTS

- 2 tablespoons olive oil
- 1 onion, finely chopped
- 2 cloves garlic, minced
- 1 red bell pepper, diced
- 1 cup short-grain rice
- 1/2 teaspoon saffron
- 1 teaspoon paprika
- 2 cups chicken broth
- 1 cup canned diced tomatoes
- 8 ounces shrimp, peeled and deveined
- 8 ounces mussels, cleaned and debearded
- 8 ounces clams, cleaned
- 1/2 cup frozen peas, thawed
- Salt and pepper to taste
- Lemon wedges and chopped parsley for garnish

Prep Time: 20 min

Cook Time: 40 min   Serves: 4

DIRECTIONS

Heat the olive oil in a large skillet or paella pan over medium heat. Add the onion, garlic, and bell pepper, and sauté until the vegetables are softened, about 5 minutes.

Stir in the rice, saffron, and paprika, cooking for another minute until the rice is well-coated with the spices.

Pour in the broth and diced tomatoes. Bring to a boil, then reduce the heat to low and simmer, covered, for 20 minutes.

Add the shrimp, mussels, and clams to the pan, tucking them into the rice. Cover and cook for 10 minutes more, or until the seafood is cooked and the shellfish have opened. Discard any shellfish that do not open.

Sprinkle the peas over the paella, cover, and cook for another 5 minutes to heat through. Season with salt and pepper to taste.

Serve the paella garnished with lemon wedges and chopped parsley.

Nutritional Information: 460 calories, 30g protein, 52g carbohydrates, 14g fat, 3g fiber, 95mg cholesterol, 540mg sodium, 500mg potassium.

Garlic Lemon Shrimp with Asparagus

INGREDIENTS

- 1-pound large shrimp, peeled and deveined
- 1 tablespoon olive oil
- 3 cloves garlic, minced
- Juice and zest of 1 lemon
- 1 pound asparagus, trimmed and cut into 2-inch pieces
- Salt and pepper to taste
- Fresh parsley, chopped, for garnish

Prep Time: 10 min

Cook Time: 10 min

Serves: 4

DIRECTIONS

Heat the olive oil in a large skillet over medium-high heat. Add the garlic and sauté until fragrant, about 1 minute. Add the shrimp to the skillet and cook until they start to turn pink, about 2-3 minutes. Add the asparagus pieces, lemon juice, and lemon zest to the skillet. Season with salt and pepper. Cook, stirring occasionally, until the shrimp are completely pink and cooked through and the asparagus is tender-crisp, about 4-5 more minutes.

Remove from heat and sprinkle with chopped parsley before serving.

Nutritional Information: 200 calories, 24g protein, 7g carbohydrates, 8g fat, 3g fiber, 150mg cholesterol, 200mg sodium, 300mg potassium.

Sardines in Tomato Sauce with Capers

INGREDIENTS

- 2 tablespoons olive oil
- 1 onion, finely chopped
- 2 cloves garlic, minced
- 1 can (14 ounces) diced tomatoes
- 1 tablespoon tomato paste
- 1/4 cup capers, rinsed
- 1/2 teaspoon crushed red pepper flakes (optional)
- 4 cans (4 ounces each) sardines in olive oil, drained
- Salt and pepper to taste
- Fresh parsley, chopped, for garnish

Prep Time: 10 min

Cook Time: 20 min

Serves: 4

DIRECTIONS

Heat the olive oil in a large skillet over medium heat. Add the onion and garlic, and sauté until the onion is translucent, about 5 minutes.

Stir in the diced tomatoes, tomato paste, capers, and red pepper flakes if using. Simmer the sauce for about 10 minutes, allowing it to thicken slightly.

Gently place the sardines in the skillet, coating them with the tomato sauce. Cook for another 5 minutes, until the sardines are heated through.

Season with salt and pepper to taste. Serve garnished with fresh parsley.

Nutritional Information: 230 calories, 23g protein, 9g carbohydrates, 13g fat, 2g fiber, 70mg cholesterol, 520mg sodium, 400mg potassium.

Greek Style Baked Cod with Lemon and Garlic

INGREDIENTS

- 4 cod fillets (about 6 ounces each)
- 3 tablespoons olive oil
- 4 cloves garlic, minced
- Juice of 1 lemon, plus extra wedges for serving
- 2 teaspoons dried oregano
- Salt and pepper to taste
- 1/4 cup chopped fresh parsley

Prep Time: 10 min

Cook Time: 15 min

Serves: 4

DIRECTIONS

Preheat the oven to 400°F (200°C). Grease a baking dish with 1 tablespoon of olive oil.

Place the cod fillets in the baking dish. In a small bowl, mix together the remaining olive oil, minced garlic, lemon juice, oregano, salt, and pepper.

Pour the garlic-lemon mixture over the cod, ensuring each fillet is well coated.

Bake in the preheated oven for about 12-15 minutes, or until the fish flakes easily with a fork.

Remove from the oven and sprinkle with chopped fresh parsley. Serve with additional lemon wedges on the side.

Nutritional Information: 210 calories, 22g protein, 3g carbohydrates, 12g fat, 1g fiber, 60mg cholesterol, 125mg sodium, 500mg potassium.

Grilled Octopus with Olive Oil and Lemon

INGREDIENTS

- 1 whole octopus (about 2 pounds), cleaned and pre-cooked
- 3 tablespoons extra virgin olive oil
- Juice of 1 lemon
- 2 cloves garlic, minced
- 1 teaspoon dried oregano
- Salt and freshly ground black pepper to taste
- Lemon wedges and chopped parsley for serving

Prep Time: 20 min

Cook Time: 10 min

Serves: 4

DIRECTIONS

If the octopus is not already pre-cooked, boil it in a large pot of salted water with a cork for about 45 minutes or until tender. Allow it to cool, then cut the tentacles and body into pieces suitable for grilling.

In a small bowl, mix together the olive oil, lemon juice, minced garlic, oregano, salt, and pepper.

Preheat the grill to medium-high heat. Brush the octopus pieces with the olive oil mixture, ensuring they are well-coated. Grill the octopus pieces for about 4-5 minutes on each side, or until charred and crispy on the edges.

Remove from the grill and transfer to a serving platter. Drizzle with a bit more olive oil and squeeze fresh lemon juice over the top. Garnish with chopped parsley and serve with additional lemon wedges.

Nutritional Information: 250 calories, 25g protein, 4g carbohydrates, 14g fat, 0g fiber, 70mg cholesterol, 480mg sodium, 350mg potassium.

Shrimp Saganaki with Feta and Tomatoes

INGREDIENTS

- 1-pound large shrimp, peeled and deveined
- 2 tablespoons olive oil
- 1 onion, finely chopped
- 3 cloves garlic, minced
- 1 can (14 ounces) diced tomatoes
- 1/4 cup dry white wine
- 1/2 teaspoon red pepper flakes
- 1/2 cup crumbled feta cheese
- 2 tablespoons fresh parsley, chopped
- Salt and pepper to taste

Prep Time: 10 min

Cook Time: 15 min

Serves: 4

DIRECTIONS

Heat olive oil in a large skillet over medium heat. Add the onion and garlic and sauté until the onion is translucent, about 5 minutes.

Stir in the diced tomatoes, white wine, and red pepper flakes. Simmer for 5 minutes to allow the flavors to meld.

Add the shrimp to the skillet and cook until they turn pink and are just cooked through, about 3-4 minutes.

Sprinkle the feta cheese over the shrimp and cover the skillet. Cook for another 2-3 minutes until the feta is slightly melted.

Season with salt and pepper to taste, then garnish with chopped parsley before serving.

Nutritional Information: 290 calories, 25g protein, 10g carbohydrates, 15g fat, 2g fiber, 180mg cholesterol, 650mg sodium, 350mg potassium.

Bouillabaisse (French Seafood Stew)

INGREDIENTS

- 1/4 cup olive oil
- 1 onion, chopped
- 2 cloves garlic, minced
- 1 leek, white part only
- 1 fennel bulb, thinly sliced
- 2 tomatoes
- 1 orange zest strip
- 1 teaspoon saffron threads
- 1 bay leaf
- 1 tablespoon thyme leaves
- 4 cups fish stock
- 1/2 pound shrimp
- 1/2 pound mussels
- 1/2 pound clams, cleaned
- 1/2 pound firm white fish
- Salt and pepper to taste

Prep Time: 20 min

Cook Time: 40 min

Serves: 4

DIRECTIONS

Start by peeling and deveining the shrimps, cleaning and debearding the mussels. Cut the white fish into chunks. Reserve all the seafood in a bowl. Slice finely the leek. Peel and dice the tomatoes.

Heat olive oil in a large pot over medium heat. Add the onion, garlic, leek, and fennel. Cook, stirring occasionally, until vegetables are softened, about 8-10 minutes. Stir in the tomatoes, orange zest, saffron, bay leaf, and thyme. Cook for another 5 minutes, then pour in the fish stock. Bring to a simmer and let cook for 20 minutes. Add the shrimp, mussels, clams, and chunks of fish to the pot. Simmer gently until the seafood is cooked and the shellfish have opened (discard any that do not open), about 10 minutes.

Season the bouillabaisse with salt and pepper to taste.

Nutritional Information: 390 calories, 35g protein, 15g carbohydrates, 18g fat, 2g fiber, 145mg cholesterol, 700mg sodium, 800mg potassium.

Scallop Risotto with Lemon and Basil

INGREDIENTS

- 1 pound sea scallops
- 2 tablespoons olive oil
- 1 small onion, finely chopped
- 2 cloves garlic, minced
- 1 cup Arborio rice
- 1/2 cup dry white wine
- 4 cups low-sodium chicken broth, kept warm
- Juice and zest of 1 lemon
- 1/2 cup fresh basil leaves, chopped
- 1/4 cup grated Parmesan cheese
- Salt and pepper to taste

Prep Time: 10 min

Cook Time: 25 min

Serves: 4

DIRECTIONS

Heat 1 tablespoon of olive oil in a large skillet over medium-high heat. Season the scallops with salt and pepper, then sear them until golden, about 2 minutes per side. Remove from the skillet and set aside. In the same skillet, add the remaining oil, onion, and garlic. Sauté until the onion is translucent, about 3 minutes. Add the rice, stirring to coat the grains in the oil. Toast the rice for 1 minute. Deglaze the pan with the white wine. Let it reduce until almost evaporated. Add the broth, one ladle at a time, stirring constantly and allowing each addition to be absorbed before adding the next. Continue until the rice is creamy and al dente, about 18-20 minutes. Stir in the lemon juice, zest, basil, and Parmesan cheese. Return the scallops to the skillet, fold gently. Adjust seasoning with salt and pepper.

Serve the risotto warm, garnished with additional basil and lemon zest if desired.

Nutritional Information: 410 calories, 26g protein, 47g carbohydrates, 12g fat, 2g fiber, 45mg cholesterol, 560mg sodium, 500mg potassium.

Ceviche with Mediterranean Flavors

INGREDIENTS

- 1-pound fresh firm white fish (such as sea bass), cut into 1/2-inch cubes
- Juice of 4 limes
- 1/4 cup olive oil
- 1 small red onion, chopped
- 1 cup cherry tomatoes
- 1/2 cup pitted Kalamata olives, halved
- 1/4 cup chopped parsley
- 1/4 cup chopped cilantro
- 2 tablespoons chopped fresh mint
- 1 cucumber, diced
- Salt and pepper to taste
- 1 avocado, diced
- Lime wedges

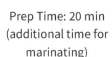

Prep Time: 20 min (additional time for marinating)

Cook Time: 0

Serves: 4

DIRECTIONS

In a non-reactive bowl, combine the fish cubes with lime juice, ensuring the fish is completely submerged. Cover and refrigerate for at least 2 hours, or until the fish becomes opaque and "cooked" in the acidity.

After the fish has marinated, drain off most of the lime juice, leaving just a small amount to keep the mixture moist. Add the olive oil, red onion, cherry tomatoes, olives, parsley, cilantro, mint, and cucumber to the fish. Toss gently to combine without breaking the fish pieces. Season with salt and pepper to taste.

Chill the ceviche in the refrigerator for an additional 30 minutes to blend the flavors. Serve the ceviche garnished with diced avocado and accompanied by lime wedges.

Nutritional Information: 310 calories, 23g protein, 15g carbohydrates, 18g fat, 5g fiber, 50mg cholesterol, 300mg sodium, 800mg potassium.

Healthy Fried Calamari with Aioli

INGREDIENTS

- 1-pound calamari, cleaned and sliced into rings
- 1/2 cup whole wheat flour
- 1 teaspoon paprika
- 1/2 teaspoon garlic powder
- Salt and pepper to taste
- Olive oil spray (for cooking)
- Lemon wedges for serving
  For the Aioli:
- 1/2 cup Greek yogurt
- 1 clove garlic, minced
- 1 tablespoon lemon juice
- 1 teaspoon olive oil
- Salt and pepper to taste

Prep Time: 15 min

Cook Time: 10 min

Serves: 4

DIRECTIONS

In a shallow dish, combine whole wheat flour, paprika, garlic powder, salt, and pepper. Dredge the calamari rings in the flour mixture until well coated.

Heat a large skillet over medium-high heat and spray generously with olive oil spray. Fry the calamari in batches, turning once, until golden and crispy, about 2 minutes per side. Remove and drain on paper towels.

For the aioli, mix Greek yogurt, minced garlic, lemon juice, olive oil, and a pinch of salt and pepper in a small bowl until smooth.

Serve the fried calamari immediately with lemon wedges and a side of the yogurt aioli for dipping.

Nutritional Information: 230 calories, 25g protein, 18g carbohydrates, 7g fat, 2g fiber, 300mg cholesterol, 250mg sodium, 350mg potassium.

Turkish Grilled Trout with Walnut Sauce

INGREDIENTS

- 4 whole trout, cleaned and gutted
- 2 tablespoons olive oil
- Salt and pepper to taste
- 1 lemon, sliced

For the Walnut Sauce:

- 1 cup walnuts, toasted
- 2 cloves garlic
- 1/4 cup bread crumbs
- 1/2 teaspoon paprika
- 1/4 teaspoon cayenne pepper
- Juice of 1 lemon
- 1/2 cup water
- Salt to taste

Prep Time: 15 min

Cook Time: 10 min

Serves: 4

DIRECTIONS

Preheat your grill to medium-high heat. Rub each trout with olive oil and season inside and out with salt and pepper. Stuff the cavity of each trout with lemon slices.

Grill the trout over medium-high heat, turning once, until the skin is crispy and the fish is cooked through, about 5 minutes per side.

For the walnut sauce, combine the toasted walnuts, garlic, bread crumbs, paprika, cayenne pepper, lemon juice, and water in a food processor. Process until smooth, adding more water if necessary to achieve a sauce-like consistency. Season with salt to taste.

Serve the grilled trout hot, drizzled with the walnut sauce.

Nutritional Information: 450 calories, 38g protein, 12g carbohydrates, 28g fat, 3g fiber, 85mg cholesterol, 350mg sodium, 700mg potassium.

Stuffed Squid with Rice and Herbs

INGREDIENTS

- 8 medium-sized squid, cleaned, tentacles reserved
- 1 cup cooked rice
- 1/4 cup fresh parsley, chopped
- 1/4 cup fresh dill, chopped
- 1/4 cup fresh mint, chopped
- 2 cloves garlic, minced
- 1 small onion, finely chopped
- 2 tablespoons olive oil, plus extra for drizzling
- 1 lemon, zest and juice
- Salt and pepper to taste
- 1 cup tomato sauce

Prep Time: 25 min

Cook Time: 35 min

Serves: 4

DIRECTIONS

Preheat the oven to 375°F (190°C).

Finely chop the reserved squid tentacles. In a skillet over medium heat, heat 1 tablespoon of olive oil. Add the onion and garlic, sautéing until translucent. Add the chopped tentacles, and cook for an additional 2-3 minutes.

In a bowl, mix the cooked rice, sautéed onion, tentacles, parsley, dill, mint, lemon zest, and half of the lemon juice. Season with salt and pepper. This will be your stuffing. Stuff each squid body with the rice mixture, and close the opening with a toothpick. Place the stuffed squid in a baking dish.

Mix the tomato sauce with the remaining olive oil and lemon juice. Pour this over the squid in the dish. Drizzle the squid with a little more olive oil, then bake in the preheated oven for about 30-35 minutes, or until the squid is tender.

Serve hot, garnished with additional herbs if desired.

Nutritional Information: 260 calories, 22g protein, 23g carbohydrates, 9g fat, 2g fiber, 320mg cholesterol, 380mg sodium, 350mg potassium.

Baked Trout with Almonds

INGREDIENTS

- 4 trout fillets (about 6 ounces each)
- 2 tablespoons olive oil
- Juice of 1 lemon
- Salt and pepper to taste
- 1/2 cup sliced almonds
- 2 tablespoons fresh parsley, chopped
- 1 garlic clove, minced
- Lemon wedges, for serving

 Prep Time: 10 min

 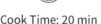 Cook Time: 20 min

 Serves: 4

DIRECTIONS

Preheat the oven to 400°F (200°C). Line a baking sheet with parchment paper or lightly grease it with cooking spray.

Place the trout fillets on the prepared baking sheet. Drizzle with olive oil and lemon juice, then season with salt and pepper.

In a small bowl, mix the sliced almonds, parsley, and minced garlic. Spread this mixture evenly over the trout fillets.

Bake in the preheated oven for about 15-20 minutes, or until the trout is cooked through and the almonds are golden and toasted.

Serve the baked trout hot, garnished with additional parsley and lemon wedges on the side.

Nutritional Information: 340 calories, 28g protein, 4g carbohydrates, 23g fat, 2g fiber, 75mg cholesterol, 180mg sodium, 500mg potassium.

Sole Meunière with Browned Butter Lemon Sauce

INGREDIENTS

- 4 sole fillets (about 6 ounces each)
- 1/4 cup all-purpose flour
- Salt and pepper to taste
- 4 tablespoons unsalted butter
- Juice of 1 lemon
- 2 tablespoons capers, drained
- 2 tablespoons fresh parsley, chopped
- Lemon wedges, for serving

 Prep Time: 10 min

 Cook Time: 10 min

 Serves: 4

DIRECTIONS

Pat the sole fillets dry with paper towels. In a shallow dish, combine the flour with salt and pepper. Dredge each fillet in the seasoned flour, shaking off any excess.

In a large skillet, melt 2 tablespoons of butter over medium heat until it starts to foam. Add the sole fillets and cook for about 2-3 minutes on each side or until golden brown and the fish flakes easily with a fork. Remove the fish from the skillet and keep warm.

In the same skillet, add the remaining 2 tablespoons of butter and cook until it turns a nutty brown color, being careful not to let it burn. Remove from heat and stir in the lemon juice and capers.

Pour the browned butter lemon sauce over the cooked sole fillets. Garnish with chopped parsley and serve immediately with lemon wedges on the side.

Nutritional Information: 280 calories, 23g protein, 8g carbohydrates, 17g fat, 1g fiber, 80mg cholesterol, 250mg sodium, 350mg potassium.

Desserts

Lemon Olive Oil Cake

INGREDIENTS

- 1 cup all-purpose flour
- 1/2 cup whole wheat flour
- 2 teaspoons baking powder
- 1/2 teaspoon salt
- 1 cup granulated sugar
- 3 large eggs
- 1/2 cup extra virgin olive oil
- Juice and zest of 2 lemons
- 1 teaspoon vanilla extract
- 1/2 cup low-fat Greek yogurt

Prep Time: 15 min

Cook Time: 35 min

Serves: 6

DIRECTIONS

Preheat your oven to 350°F (175°C). Grease a 9-inch cake pan and line the bottom with parchment paper.

In a medium bowl, whisk together both flours, baking powder, and salt. In a large bowl, whisk the sugar and eggs until light and fluffy. Gradually whisk in the olive oil, followed by the lemon juice and zest, and vanilla extract. Alternately fold in the flour mixture and Greek yogurt into the egg mixture. Mix until just combined. Pour the batter into the prepared cake pan and smooth the top with a spatula. Bake in the oven for about 35 minutes or until a toothpick inserted into the center of the cake comes out clean. Let the cake cool in the pan for 10 minutes, then turn out onto a wire rack to cool completely.

Nutritional Information: 430 calories, 7g protein, 53g carbohydrates, 22g fat, 1g fiber, 106mg cholesterol, 340mg sodium, 98mg potassium.

Ricotta and Honey Stuffed Figs

INGREDIENTS

- 8 fresh figs, stemmed and halved
- 1/2 cup ricotta cheese
- 2 tablespoons honey
- 1/4 teaspoon ground cinnamon
- 2 tablespoons chopped walnuts or pistachios, optional

Prep Time: 10 min

Cook Time: 0 min

Serves: 4

DIRECTIONS

In a small bowl, mix together the ricotta cheese, honey, and ground cinnamon. Using a small spoon, carefully scoop out a small amount of flesh from the center of each fig half to create a hollow. Spoon the ricotta mixture into the hollowed-out center of each fig half, dividing evenly among them. If desired, sprinkle chopped walnuts or pistachios over the stuffed figs for added crunch and flavor. Arrange the stuffed figs on a serving platter and drizzle with a little extra honey if desired. Serve immediately.

Nutritional Information: 120 calories, 3g protein, 20g carbohydrates, 4g fat, 3g fiber, 8mg cholesterol, 45mg sodium, 240mg potassium.

Grilled Peaches with Honey and Yogurt

INGREDIENTS

- 4 ripe peaches, halved and pitted
- 1 tablespoon honey
- 1 cup Greek yogurt
- 1 tablespoon chopped fresh mint (optional)

 Prep Time: 5 min

 Cook Time: 6 min

 Serves: 4

DIRECTIONS

Preheat your grill to medium-high heat.

Brush the cut sides of the peach halves lightly with honey.

Place the peaches, cut side down, on the grill grates and cook for about 3 minutes, or until grill marks appear.

Flip the peaches over and continue to grill for another 2-3 minutes, or until they are tender but still hold their shape.

Remove the grilled peaches from the grill and let them cool slightly.

Serve the grilled peaches with a dollop of Greek yogurt on top.

Garnish with chopped fresh mint, if desired, for extra flavor and freshness.

Nutritional Information: 100 calories, 4g protein, 20g carbohydrates, 1g fat, 2g fiber, 0mg cholesterol, 20mg sodium, 300mg potassium.

Apricot and Almond Tart

INGREDIENTS

- 1 sheet frozen puff pastry, thawed
- 1/2 cup almond flour
- 1/4 cup granulated sugar
- 1/4 teaspoon almond extract
- 1/4 cup unsalted butter, melted
- 6 ripe apricots, halved and pitted
- 2 tablespoons sliced almonds
- Powdered sugar, for dusting (optional)

 Prep Time: 15 min

 Cook Time: 30 min

 Serves: 6

DIRECTIONS

Preheat your oven to 375°F (190°C). Line a baking sheet with parchment paper.

Roll out the puff pastry sheet on a lightly floured surface to fit the size of your baking sheet. Transfer the pastry to the prepared baking sheet.

In a small bowl, mix together the almond flour, granulated sugar, almond extract, and melted butter until well combined.

Spread the almond mixture evenly over the puff pastry, leaving a small border around the edges.

Arrange the apricot halves, cut side up, on top of the almond mixture.

Sprinkle the sliced almonds over the apricots.

Bake in the preheated oven for 25-30 minutes, or until the pastry is golden brown and the apricots are tender.

Remove from the oven and let the tart cool slightly before serving.

Dust with powdered sugar, if desired, before serving.

Nutritional Information: 275 calories, 4g protein, 24g carbohydrates, 18g fat, 2g fiber, 15mg cholesterol, 90mg sodium, 300mg potassium.

Fresh Berry and Mint Salad

INGREDIENTS

- 2 cups mixed fresh berries (such as strawberries, blueberries, raspberries, and blackberries)
- 2 tablespoons fresh mint leaves, chopped
- 1 tablespoon honey
- 1 tablespoon fresh lemon juice
- Zest of 1 lemon

 Prep Time: 10 min

 Cook Time: 0 min

 Serves: 4

DIRECTIONS

Rinse the mixed berries under cold water and pat them dry with paper towels. If using strawberries, hull and slice them.

In a large bowl, gently toss the mixed berries with the chopped fresh mint leaves.

In a small bowl, whisk together the honey, fresh lemon juice, and lemon zest until well combined.

Drizzle the honey-lemon dressing over the mixed berries and mint, and toss gently to coat.

Serve immediately or refrigerate until ready to serve.

Nutritional Information: 70 calories, 1g protein, 18g carbohydrates, 0g fat, 3g fiber, 0mg cholesterol, 0mg sodium, 150mg potassium.

Baked Apples with Cinnamon and Nuts

INGREDIENTS

- 4 medium-sized apples (such as Granny Smith or Honeycrisp)
- 2 tablespoons chopped nuts (such as walnuts or pecans)
- 2 tablespoons honey
- 1 teaspoon ground cinnamon
- 1 tablespoon unsalted butter, melted
- Pinch of salt

  Prep Time: 10 min

 Cook Time: 30 min

 Serves: 4

DIRECTIONS

Preheat your oven to 375°F (190°C). Lightly grease a baking dish with non-stick cooking spray or butter.

Wash and core the apples, then use a paring knife to score a shallow cut around the circumference of each apple to prevent splitting while baking.

In a small bowl, mix together the chopped nuts, honey, ground cinnamon, melted butter, and a pinch of salt until well combined.

Place the cored apples in the prepared baking dish. Fill each apple cavity with the nut and honey mixture, pressing it down gently.

Bake the apples in the preheated oven for about 25-30 minutes, or until the apples are tender and the filling is golden brown and bubbling.

Remove the baked apples from the oven and let them cool slightly before serving.

Nutritional Information: 150 calories, 1g protein, 30g carbohydrates, 4g fat, 5g fiber, 5mg cholesterol, 0mg sodium, 250mg potassium.

Chocolate and Olive Oil Mousse

INGREDIENTS

- 4 ounces dark chocolate, chopped
- 1/4 cup extra virgin olive oil
- 2 tablespoons honey or maple syrup
- 1 teaspoon vanilla extract
- Pinch of salt
- Fresh berries, for serving (optional)
- Mint leaves, for garnish (optional)

 Prep Time: 10 min

 Cook Time: 0 min

 Serves: 4

DIRECTIONS

In a heatproof bowl set over a pot of simmering water, melt the dark chocolate, stirring occasionally until smooth and melted. Remove from heat and let it cool slightly.

Once the melted chocolate has cooled slightly, whisk in the extra virgin olive oil, honey or maple syrup, vanilla extract, and a pinch of salt until well combined and smooth.

Divide the chocolate mixture evenly among serving glasses or ramekins. Smooth the tops with a spatula or back of a spoon.

Cover the glasses with plastic wrap and refrigerate for at least 2 hours, or until the mousse is set.

Before serving, garnish with fresh berries and mint leaves if desired.

Nutritional Information: 250 calories, 2g protein, 18g carbohydrates, 20g fat, 3g fiber, 0mg cholesterol, 50mg sodium, 150mg potassium.

Cannoli with Ricotta and Pistachios

INGREDIENTS

- 12 cannoli shells
- 1 cup part-skim ricotta cheese
- 1/4 cup powdered sugar
- 1 teaspoon vanilla extract
- Zest of 1 lemon
- 1/4 cup chopped pistachios, plus extra for garnish
- Dark chocolate chips, for garnish (optional)

 Prep Time: 30 min

 Cook Time: 10 min

 Serves: 6

DIRECTIONS

In a mixing bowl, combine the ricotta cheese, powdered sugar, vanilla extract, and lemon zest. Mix well until smooth and creamy.

Fold in the chopped pistachios until evenly distributed throughout the ricotta mixture.

Fill each cannoli shell with the ricotta and pistachio mixture using a spoon or piping bag, ensuring they are evenly filled from end to end.

Garnish the ends of the cannoli with extra chopped pistachios and dark chocolate chips if desired.

Serve immediately or refrigerate until ready to serve.

Nutritional Information: 210 calories, 6g protein, 20g carbohydrates, 11g fat, 1g fiber, 15mg cholesterol, 85mg sodium, 150mg potassium.

Date and Walnut Balls (Energy Bites)

INGREDIENTS

- 1 cup pitted dates
- 1/2 cup walnuts
- 2 tablespoons unsweetened shredded coconut
- 1 tablespoon chia seeds
- 1/2 teaspoon ground cinnamon

Prep Time: 15 min

Cook Time: 0 min

Serves: 4

DIRECTIONS

In a food processor, combine the pitted dates, walnuts, shredded coconut, chia seeds, and ground cinnamon.

Pulse the mixture until it forms a sticky dough-like consistency and the ingredients are well combined.

Scoop out tablespoon-sized portions of the mixture and roll them into balls using your hands.

Place the rolled balls on a plate or baking sheet lined with parchment paper.

Once all the mixture is rolled into balls, refrigerate them for at least 30 minutes to firm up before serving.

Nutritional Information: 120 calories, 2g protein, 18g carbohydrates, 6g fat, 3g fiber, 0mg cholesterol, 0mg sodium, 150mg potassium.

Orange and Almond Flan

INGREDIENTS

- 3 large eggs
- 1/4 cup honey
- 1/2 cup almond milk
- Zest of 1 orange
- 1/4 teaspoon almond extract
- 1/4 cup almond flour
- Sliced almonds, for garnish

Prep Time: 15 min

Cook Time: 35 min

Serves: 4

DIRECTIONS

Preheat the oven to 350°F (175°C). Grease four ramekins with cooking spray and place them on a baking sheet.

In a mixing bowl, whisk together the eggs and honey until well combined.

Add the almond milk, orange zest, and almond extract to the egg mixture, and whisk until smooth.

Gradually whisk in the almond flour until the batter is smooth and slightly thickened.

Divide the batter evenly among the prepared ramekins. Sprinkle sliced almonds on top of each flan.

Bake in the preheated oven for 30-35 minutes, or until the flans are set and golden brown on top.

Remove from the oven and let cool slightly before serving.

Nutritional Information: 190 calories, 7g protein, 17g carbohydrates, 11g fat, 2g fiber, 140mg cholesterol, 65mg sodium, 180mg potassium.

Tiramisu with Greek Yogurt

INGREDIENTS

- 1 cup Greek yogurt
- 1/4 cup honey
- 1 teaspoon vanilla extract
- 1/2 cup brewed coffee, cooled
- 2 tablespoons coffee liqueur (optional)
- 8 ladyfinger cookies
- Cocoa powder, for dusting

 Prep Time: 20 min

 Cook Time: 0 min

 Serves: 4

DIRECTIONS

In a mixing bowl, combine the Greek yogurt, honey, and vanilla extract. Mix until smooth and well combined.

In a shallow dish, mix the cooled brewed coffee with coffee liqueur (if using).

Quickly dip each ladyfinger cookie into the coffee mixture, ensuring they are soaked but not soggy.

Arrange a layer of soaked ladyfinger cookies at the bottom of serving glasses or a baking dish. Spoon half of the Greek yogurt mixture over the ladyfingers, spreading it evenly. Repeat with another layer of soaked ladyfingers and the remaining Greek yogurt mixture.

Cover and refrigerate for at least 2 hours, or until set.

Before serving, dust the top of the tiramisu with cocoa powder.

Nutritional Information: 190 calories, 8g protein, 29g carbohydrates, 5g fat, 1g fiber, 20mg cholesterol, 50mg sodium, 150mg potassium.

Citrus Salad with Honey and Mint

INGREDIENTS

- 2 oranges
- 2 grapefruits
- 1 tablespoon honey
- 2 tablespoons fresh mint leaves, chopped
- 1 tablespoon lime juice
- 1/4 cup chopped pistachios (optional)
- Fresh mint leaves, for garnish

 Prep Time: 15 min

 Cook Time: 0 min

 Serves: 4

DIRECTIONS

Peel the oranges and grapefruits, removing the white pith, and slice them into thin rounds or segments.

Arrange the citrus slices on a serving platter or individual plates.

In a small bowl, whisk together the honey, chopped mint leaves, and lime juice to make the dressing.

Drizzle the honey and mint dressing over the citrus slices.

Sprinkle chopped pistachios (if using) over the salad.

Garnish with fresh mint leaves.

Serve immediately or chill in the refrigerator until ready to serve.

Nutritional Information: 120 calories, 2g protein, 28g carbohydrates, 2g fat, 4g fiber, 0mg cholesterol, 0mg sodium, 400mg potassium.

Meal plan for 30 days

	Breakfast	Lunch	Snack	Dinner
Day 1	Olive Oil and Tomato Toast - *Page 19*	Greek Potato Salad + Pork Tenderloin with Herbs and Garlic -*Page 34 + Page 83*	Lemon Olive Oil Cake - *Page 102*	Greek Gigantes Plaki - *Page 61*
Day 2	Greek Yogurt with Honey and Walnuts - *Page 23*	Greek Lemon Chicken Soup (Avgolemono) - *Page 50*	Stuffed Grape Leaves (Dolma) - *Page 36*	Grilled Chicken with Tzatziki Sauce - *Page 81*
Day 3	Shakshuka - *Page 20*	Greek Lemon Rice + Grilled Salmon with Olive Tapenade - *Page 67 + Page 91*	Ricotta and Honey Stuffed Figs - *Page 102*	Moroccan Carrot Salad + Spicy Moroccan Chicken with Preserved Lemons - *Page 30 + Page 86*
Day 4	Date and Nut Porridge - *Page 24*	Penne with Chickpeas, Spinach & Tomatoes - *Page 73*	Caponata Salad - *Page 30*	Italian Minestrone Soup - *Page 51*
Day 5	Spinach and Feta Phyllo Pie - *Page 21*	Italian Pasta e Fagioli - *Page 62*	Grilled Peaches with Honey and Yogurt - *Page 103*	Chicken Souvlaki with Lemon and Oregano - *Page 82*
Day 6	Fig and Honey Toast - *Page 24*	Couscous with Roasted Vegetables + Braised Chicken with Capers and Olives - *Page 68 + Page 87*	Baba Ganoush - *Page 35*	Grilled Mackerel with Salad Greens - *Page 93*
Day 7	Grilled Halloumi Cheese with Lemon - *Page 19*	Mediterranean Quinoa Salad - *Page 32*	Apricot and Almond Tart - *Page 103*	Stuffed Bell Peppers with Ground Beef and Herbs - *Page 82*
Day 8	Pomegranate and Pistachio Müesli - *Page 25*	Greek Fisherman's Soup (Kakavia) - *Page 56*	Mediterranean Chickpea Salad - *Page 31*	Couscous Stuffed Bell Peppers - *Page 72*
Day 9	Tomato and Olive Tapenade on Whole Grain Bread - *Page 20*	Spanish Lentil Stew with Chorizo - *Page 62*	Cannoli with Ricotta and Pistachios - *Page 105*	Chicken Shawarma with Yogurt Sauce - *Page 88*
Day 10	Orange and Polenta Cake - *Page 25*	Greek Style Baked Cod with Lemon and Garlic + Mediterranean Rice Pilaf - *Page 96 + Page 69*	Muhammara - *Page 38*	Greek Pasta Salad with Cucumber, Feta, and Olives - *Page 75*
Day 11	Hummus Rolls with Vegetables - *Page 22*	Chicken and Artichoke Paella - *Page 88*	Fresh Berry and Mint Salad - *Page 104*	Spanish Gazpacho - *Page 51*
Day 12	Honey-Sweetened Ricotta with Berries - *Page 26*	Greek Fava Santorinis + Moroccan Spiced Chicken with Dried Apricots - *Page 65 + Page 90*	Italian Panzanella - *Page 29*	Tabbouleh - *Page 28*
Day 13	Turkish Menemen - *Page 22*	Scallop Risotto with Lemon and Basil - *Page 98*	Baked Apples with Cinnamon and Nuts - *Page 104*	Linguine with Zucchini, Mint, and Almonds - *Page 78*
Day 14	Berry and Mascarpone Bruschetta - *Page 26*	Lebanese Lentil Salad - *Page 31*	Artichoke Hearts with Vinaigrette - *Page 39*	Lamb Gyros with Cucumber Yogurt Sauce - *Page 87*

Day 15	Italian Frittata with Zucchini and Goat Cheese - *Page 23*	Turkish Chicken and Vegetable Soup - *Page 58*	Chocolate and Olive Oil Mousse - *Page 105*	Spanish Garbanzos con Espinacas - *Page 66*
Day 16	Apricot and Walnut Stuffed Crepes - *Page 27*	Chicken Gyros with Cucumber Salsa and Tsatsiki - *Page 89*	Mediterranean Quinoa Salad - *Page 32*	Italian Tomato Risotto + Turkey Meatballs in Tomato Basil Sauce - *Page 71 + Page 81*
Day 17	Lebanese Labneh with Olive Tapenade - *Page 21*	Seafood Paella - *Page 95*	Date and Walnut Balls - *Page 106*	Baked Penne with Eggplant and Mozzarella - *Page 80*
Day 18	Cherry and Almond Oatmeal - *Page 27*	Fattoush Salad - *Page 29*	Hummus - *Page 35*	Italian Beef Braciole Stuffed with Herbs and Cheese - *Page 85*
Day 19	Olive Oil and Tomato Toast - *Page 19*	Moroccan Tomato Soup with Chickpeas and Rice - *Page 57*	Orange and Almond Flan - *Page 106*	Greek Fasolakia (Green Bean Stew) - *Page 63*
Day 20	Greek Yogurt with Honey and Walnuts - *Page 23*	Stuffed Chicken Breasts with Feta and Spinach + Israeli Couscous with Herbs - *Page 80*	Balela Salad - *Page 32*	Grilled Sea Bass with Garlic and Herbs - *Page 94*
Day 21	Shakshuka - *Page 20*	Fusilli with Spinach and Ricotta Sauce - *Page 76*	Tiramisu with Greek Yogurt - *Page 107*	Lebanese Lentil Salad - *Page 31*
Day 22	Date and Nut Porridge - *Page 24*	Moroccan Lamb Tagine with Prunes and Almonds - *Page 83*	Falafel - *Page 37*	Spanish Gazpacho - *Page 51*
Day 23	Spinach and Feta Phyllo Pie - *Page 21*	Spanish Lentil Stew with Chorizo - *Page 62*	Citrus Salad with Honey and Mint - *Page 107*	Chicken Souvlaki with Lemon and Oregano - *Page 82*
Day 24	Fig and Honey Toast - *Page 24*	Couscous Stuffed Bell Peppers - *Page 72*	Watermelon and Feta Salad - *Page 33*	Grilled Octopus with Olive Oil and Lemon - *Page 97*
Day 25	Grilled Halloumi Cheese with Lemon - *Page 19*	Whole Wheat Spaghetti with Arugula Pesto + Roasted Chicken with Mediterranean Herb Rub - *Page 77 + Page 84*	Grilled Peaches with Honey and Yogurt - *Page 103*	Greek Salad (Horiatiki) - *Page 28*
Day 26	Pomegranate and Pistachio Müesli - *Page 25*	Stuffed Squid with Rice and Herbs - *Page 100*	Tzatziki - *Page 36*	Ceviche with Mediterranean Flavors - *Page 99*
Day 27	Tomato and Olive Tapenade on Whole Grain Bread - *Page 20*	Greek Moussaka with Ground Lamb - *Page 85*	Apricot and Almond Tart - *Page 103*	Baked Stuffed Tomatoes with Rice - *Page 70*
Day 28	Orange and Polenta Cake - *Page 25*	Bouillabaisse (French Seafood Stew) - *Page 98*	Fattoush Salad - *Page 29*	Farro Risotto with Mushrooms - *Page 71*
Day 29	Hummus Rolls with Vegetables - *Page 22*	Garlic Lemon Shrimp with Asparagus + Italian Tomato Risotto - *Page 95 + Page 71*	Ricotta and Honey Stuffed Figs - *Page 102*	Vegetable Pasta Primavera with Whole Wheat Fusilli - *Page 74*
Day 30	Honey-Sweetened Ricotta with Berries - *Page 26*	Italian Polenta with Tomato Sauce + Stuffed Bell Peppers with Ground Beef and Herbs - *Page 70 + Page 82*	Greek Salad (Horiatiki) - *Page 28*	Fish Stew with Tomatoes and Fennel - *Page 93*

Made in the USA
Las Vegas, NV
08 March 2025

19251410R00063